JUHANI PALLASMAA

THE EYES OF THE SKIN

ARCHITECTURE AND THE SENSES

FOURTH EDITION

WILEY

This edition first published 2024

Edition History: John Wiley & Sons Ltd (3e, 2012)

Registered Offices
John Wiley & Sons, Inc., 111 River Street, Hoboken, NJ 07030, USA
John Wiley & Sons Ltd, The Atrium, Southern Gate, Chichester, West Sussex, PO19 8SQ, UK

For details of our global editorial offices, customer services, and more information about Wiley products visit us at www.wiley.com.

Wiley also publishes its books in a variety of electronic formats and by print-on-demand. Some content that appears in standard print versions of this book may not be available in other formats.

Library of Congress Cataloging-in-Publication Data

Names: Pallasmaa, Juhani, author.
Title: The eyes of the skin : architecture and the senses / Juhani Pallasmaa.
Description: Fourth edition. | Hoboken, NJ : Wiley, 2024. | Includes index.
Identifiers: LCCN 2023034968 (print) | LCCN 2023034969 (ebook) | ISBN 9781394200672 (cloth) | ISBN 9781394200696 (adobe pdf) | ISBN 9781394200689 (epub)
Subjects: LCSH: Architecture—Philosophy. | Senses and sensation in architecture.
Classification: LCC NA2500 .P35 2024 (print) | LCC NA2500 (ebook) | DDC 720.1—dc23/eng/20231206
LC record available at https://lccn.loc.gov/2023034968
LC ebook record available at https://lccn.loc.gov/2023034969

Cover Design and Image: Wiley

Set in 9/11.5pt Bembo Std by Straive, Chennai, India

SKY10094827_123024

CONTENTS

FOREWORD		vi
INTRODUCTION	Touching the World by *Juhani Pallasmaa*	2
PART ONE	Vision and Knowledge	10
	Critics of Ocularcentrism	14
	The Narcissistic and Nihilistic Eye	16
	Oral Versus Visual Space	17
	Retinal Architecture and the Loss of Plasticity	20
	An Architecture of Visual Images	24
	Materiality and Time	25
	The Rejection of Alberti's Window	28
	A New Vision and Sensory Balance	30
PART TWO	The Body in the Centre	33
	Multi-Sensory Experience	34
	The Significance of the Shadow	39
	Acoustic Intimacy	42
	Silence, Time and Solitude	43
	Spaces of Scent	46
	The Shape of Touch	48
	The Taste of Stone	50
	Images of Muscle and Bone	51
	Images of Action	54
	Bodily Identification	55
	Mimesis of the Body	56
	Spaces of Memory and Imagination	60
	An Architecture of the Senses	61
	The Task of Architecture	62
A DOOR HANDLE, A HANDSHAKE	An introduction to Juhani Pallasmaa and his work by *Peter MacKeith*	64
	Apertures	72
	Poetics	81
NOTES		88
INDEX		99
PICTURE CREDITS		103

THIN
ICE
STEVEN
HOLL

Foreword

When I sat down to write these notes in rainy New York City, thinking of the fresh white snow which had just fallen in Helsinki and the early thin ice, I remembered stories of Finland's cold winter, where every year short-cut roads are improvised across the thickly frozen north lakes. Months later as the ice begins to thin, someone will take the gamble to drive across the lake and crash through. I imagine the last look out over white ice cracks spread by cold black water rising up inside the sinking car. Finland's is a tragic and mysterious beauty.

Juhani Pallasmaa and I first began to share thoughts about the phenomenology of architecture during my first visit to Finland for the 5th Alvar Aalto Symposium in Jyväskylä in August 1991.

In October 1992, we met again in Helsinki when I was there to work on the competition for the Museum of Contemporary Art. I remember a conversation about Maurice Merleau-Ponty's writings as they might be interpreted or directed towards spatial sequence, texture, material and light, experienced in architecture. I recall this conversation took place over lunch below decks in a huge wooden boat anchored in the Helsinki harbour. The steam rose in curls above the vegetable soup as the boat rocked slightly in the partially frozen harbour. I have experienced the architecture of Juhani Pallasmaa, from his wonderful museum additions at Rovaniemi to his wooden summerhouse on a remarkable little stone island in the Turku Archipelago in southwestern Finland. The way spaces feel, the sound and smell of these places, has equal weight to the way things look. Pallasmaa is not just a theoretician; he is a brilliant architect of phenomenological insight. He practises the unanalysable architecture of the senses whose phenomenal properties concretise his writings towards a philosophy of architecture.

In 1993, following an invitation from Toshio Nakamura, we worked together with Alberto Pérez-Gómez to produce the book *Questions of Perception: Phenomenology of Architecture.*[1] Several years later the publishers, A+U, chose to republish this little book, finding its arguments proved important to other architects.

Juhani Pallasmaa's *The Eyes of the Skin,* which grew out of *Questions of Perception,* is a tighter, clearer argument for the crucial phenomenological dimensions of human experience in architecture. Not since the Danish architect Steen Eiler Rasmussen's *Experiencing Architecture* (1959) has there been such a succinct and clear text which could serve students and architects at this critical time in the development of 21st-century architecture.[2]

Merleau-Ponty's *The Visible and the Invisible,* the book he was writing when he died, contains an astonishing chapter: 'The Intertwining – The Chiasm'. (It was, in fact, the source of the name I gave my 1992 competition entry for the Museum of Contemporary Art in Helsinki – Chiasm was changed to Kiasma, there being no 'C' in Finnish.) In the chapter's text on the 'Horizon of Things', Merleau-Ponty wrote: 'No more than are the sky or the earth is the horizon a collection of things held together, or a class name, or a logical possibility of conception, or a system of "potentiality of consciousness": it is a new type of being, a being by porosity, pregnancy, or generality . . .'.[3]

In the second decade of the 21st century, these thoughts go beyond the horizon and 'beneath the skin'. Throughout our world, consumer goods propelled by hyperbolic advertising techniques serve to supplant our consciousness and diffuse our reflective capacity. In architecture, the application of new, digitally supercharged techniques currently joins the hyperbole. With this noisy background, the work of Pallasmaa evokes reflective solitude and resolve – what he has once called 'The Architecture of Silence'. I will urge my students to read this work and reflect on 'background noise'. Today, the 'depth of our being' stands on thin ice.

TOUCHING THE WORLD

JUHANI PALLASMAA

Introduction

My little book *The Eyes of the Skin: Architecture and the Senses* was first published in 1996 in the 'Polemics' series of Academy Editions, London. The editors of the series invited me to write an extended essay of 32 pages on a subject matter that I found pertinent in the architectural discourse of the time.

The second part of the manuscript took its basic ideas from an essay entitled 'An Architecture of the Seven Senses', published in the July 1994 special edition of *A+U* entitled *Questions of Perception*, a publication on Steven Holl's architectural work, which also included essays by Holl himself and Alberto Pérez-Gómez. A somewhat later lecture of mine given in a seminar on architectural phenomenology at the Royal Danish Academy of Fine Arts in Copenhagen in June 1995, where the three writers of *Questions of Perception* presented lectures, provided the basic arguments and references for the first part of this book.

Somewhat to my surprise, the humble book was received very positively, and it became required reading in architectural theory courses in numerous schools of architecture around the world.

The polemical essay was initially based on my personal experiences, views and speculations. I had simply become increasingly concerned about the dominance of vision and the suppression of other senses in the way architecture was taught, conceived and critiqued, and the consequent disappearance of sensory and sensual qualities from architecture.

As this new edition was first discussed between the publisher and myself, I was hesitant to expand my text of the original edition, as I consider the original edition a historical document, which is grounded in the understanding and thinking of the senses at the time the book was written, more than a quarter of a century ago. However, I agreed to make minor corrections and clarifications, which do not alter the original arguments, but make them easier to understand. The additions also intentionally expand the original arguments beyond the senses to the existential sphere of architecture.

During the years since I wrote the book, interest in the significance of the senses, both philosophically and in terms of experiencing, teaching and making architecture, has grown significantly. My assumptions about the role of the body as the locus of perception, thought and consciousness, as well as about the significance of the senses in articulating, storing and processing sensory responses and thoughts, have been strengthened and confirmed by other writers. In particular, philosophical investigations on human embodiment, experience and atmospheres, as well as recent neurological research on the senses, have provided support for my assumptions.

In the 28 years since the first publication of the book, my thinking has deepened and widened. For instance, I have understood the significance of atmospheres in our multisensory experiences and evaluations of environments and architecture.

With the choice of the title 'The Eyes of the Skin', I wished to express the significance of the tactile sense for our experience and understanding of the world, but I also intended to create a conceptual short circuit between the dominant sense of vision and the suppressed sense modality of touch. Later, in a conversation with the American light artist, James Turrell, I learned that our skin is capable of distinguishing a number of colours; we actually do see by our skin.[1]

The significance of the tactile sense in human life has become increasingly evident. The view of Ashley Montagu, the anthropologist, based on medical evidence, confirms the primacy of the haptic realm:

> [The skin] is the oldest and the most sensitive of our organs, our first medium of communication, and our most efficient protector [. . .] Even the transparent cornea of the eye is overlain by a layer of modified skin [. . .] Touch is the parent of our eyes, ears, nose, and mouth. It is the sense which became differentiated into the others, a fact that seems to be recognized in the age-old evaluation of touch as 'the mother of the senses'.[2]

Touch is the sensory mode which integrates our experiences of the world and of ourselves. Even visual perceptions are fused and integrated into the haptic continuum of the self; my body remembers who I am and how I am located in the world. My body is truly the navel of my world, not in the sense of the viewing point of the central perspective, but as the very locus of reference, memory, imagination and integration. All the senses, including vision, are, in a way, extensions of the tactile sense; the senses are specialisations of skin tissue, and all sensory experiences are modes of touching, and thus related to tactility. Our contact with the world takes place at the boundary line of the self through specialised parts of our enveloping membrane. We humans, just as all animals, are extending ourselves into the world through our actions as well as material and mental constructions. As representatives of Homo sapience, our image of self does not stop at the skin, as we relate and extend ourselves in countless ways by means of mobility, technology, materials, culture and beliefs, both scientific and religious.

It is evident that 'life-enhancing'[3] architecture has to address all the senses simultaneously, and help to fuse our image of self with our experience of the world. Architecture is fundamentally a relational art; it relates us with both the intimacies and immensities of the world. The essential mental task of buildings is relational accommodation and integration. They project our human measures and sense of order into the measureless and meaningless natural space. Architecture does not make us inhabit worlds of mere fabrication and fantasy; it articulates the experience of our being-in-the-world and strengthens our sense of reality and self. Most importantly, it projects experiential meaning to our existence in the world.

The sense of self, strengthened by art and architecture, also permits us to engage fully in the mental dimensions of dream, imagination and desire. Buildings and cities provide the horizon for the understanding and confronting of the human existential condition. Instead of creating mere objects of visual seduction, architecture relates, mediates and projects meanings. The ultimate meaning of any building is beyond architecture; it directs our consciousness back to the world and towards our own sense of self and being. Profound architecture makes us experience ourselves as complete, embodied and spiritual beings. In fact, this is the great function of all meaningful art.

In the experience of art, a peculiar exchange takes place; I lend my emotions and associations to the place, and the place lends me its atmosphere, which entices and emancipates my perceptions and thoughts. An architectural work is not experienced as a series of isolated retinal pictures, but in its full and integrated material, embodied and spiritual essence. It offers pleasurable shapes and surfaces moulded for the touch of the eye and the other senses, but it also incorporates and integrates physical and mental structures, giving our existential experience a strengthened coherence and significance.

In creative work, the artist, craftsman and architect are directly engaged with their bodies and their existential experiences rather than focusing on an external and objectified problem. True artistic works are always relational entities, fusing and integrating our external and internal worlds, our bodily experiences and mental imageries. The message and value of a piece of sculpture or an architectural structure is not in its material existence, but in the poetic experiences and emotions that it mediates of our life world and its meanings.

A wise architect, also, works with his/her entire body and sense of self. While working on a building or an object, the architect is simultaneously engaged in a reverse perspective, his/her self-image, or more precisely, existential experience. In creative work, a powerful identification and projection takes place; the entire bodily and mental constitution of the maker becomes the site of the work. Ludwig Wittgenstein acknowledges the interaction of both philosophical and architectural work with the image of self: 'Working in philosophy – like work in architecture in many respects – is really more a work on oneself. On one's own interpretation. On how one sees things [. . .]'.[4]

The computer is usually seen as a solely beneficial invention, which liberates human fantasy. I wish to express my serious concern in this respect, at least considering the current role of the computer in education and the design process. Computer imaging tends to flatten our magnificent, multisensory, simultaneous and synchronic capacities of imagination by turning the design process into a passive visual manipulation, a retinal journey. Design is not merely a rational, technical and performative task; architecture relates us to the course and depth of culture and makes our existence understandable. Architecture helps us give human existence its human as well as metaphysical meaning; we do not dwell only in space, place and time; we also dwell in hidden myths and spirit. Existence and life are not abstractions, and the task of the art of building is to clarify and relate human existence and give it meanings that exceed the mundane.

The computer creates a distance between the maker and the object, whereas drawing by hand as well as working with models put the designer in a haptic contact with the object, or space. When drawing, we touch the object and hold it in our hands. In our imagination, the object is simultaneously held in the hand and inside the head, and the imagined and projected physical image is modelled by our embodied imagination. We are inside and outside of the conceived object at the same time. Creative work calls for a bodily and mental identification, empathy and compassion. Recent research on mirror neurons provides an experimental basis for the understanding of the complex processes of embodied simulation.[5]

Existence and life are not abstractions, and the task of the art of building is to clarify and relate human existence and give it meanings that exceed the mundane.

We tend to think of the sense of vision only as the focused vision. However, the role of peripheral and unfocused vision in our lived experience of the world, as well as in our experience of interiority in the spaces we inhabit, has evoked my interest. A remarkable factor in the experience of enveloping spatiality, interiority and hapticity is the deliberate suppression of sharp, focused vision. This issue has hardly entered the theoretical discourse of architecture as architectural theorising continues to be interested in focused vision, pure and clear form, conscious intentionality and perspectival representation. The very essence of the lived experience is moulded by unconscious haptic imagery and unfocused peripheral vision. Focused vision confronts us with the world, whereas peripheral vision envelops us in 'the flesh of the world', to use an expression of Merleau-Ponty. Alongside the critique of the hegemony of vision, we need to reconsider the very essence of sight itself and the essential collaboration of the various sensory realms.

Photographed architectural images are centralised images of focused Gestalt. Yet, the quality of an architectural reality seems to depend fundamentally on peripheral vision, which enfolds the subject in the space. A forest context and richly moulded architectural spaces provide ample stimuli for peripheral vision, and these settings centre us in the very place, both material and experiential. The preconscious perceptual realm, which is experienced outside the sphere of focused vision, seems to be more important existentially than the focused image. In fact, there is medical evidence that peripheral vision has a higher priority in our perceptual and mental system.[6]

These observations suggest that one of the reasons why the architectural and urban settings of our time tend to make us outsiders, in comparison with the forceful emotional engagement of natural and historical settings, is their poverty of the field of peripheral vision. Unconscious peripheral perception transforms retinal Gestalt into spatial and bodily experiences. Peripheral vision integrates us with space, while focused vision pushes us out of the space, making us mere spectators.

Architectural theorising, education and practices have primarily been concerned with form. Yet, we have an astonishing capacity to perceive and grasp unconsciously and peripherally complex environmental entities and atmospheres. Atmospheric characteristics of spaces, places and settings are grasped before any conscious observation of details is made. Despite the obvious importance of atmospheric perception, it has hardly been introduced in architectural discourse. Again, neurological investigations suggest that our processes of perception and cognition advance from the instantaneous grasp of entities towards the identification of details, rather than the other way round.

Since writing *The Eyes of the Skin* 28 years ago, I have expanded my critical analysis of the neglect of the embodied essence of perception, cognition and consciousness in two later books also published by John Wiley & Sons: *The Thinking Hand: Existential and Embodied Wisdom in Architecture* (Chichester, 2009) and *The Embodied Image: Imagination and Imagery in Architecture* (Chichester, 2011). My next book *Rootedness: reflections for young architects*, currently in the editorial process at Wiley, is more deeply engaged in the existential issues of architecture, as well as of studying and practising this significant craft.

(Introduction revised, Enäjärvi Lake, Finland, June–July 2023)

PART ONE

'The hands want to see, the eyes want to caress'.
Johann Wolfgang von Goethe[1]

'The dancer has his ear in his toes'.
Friedrich Nietzsche[2]

'If the body had been easier to understand, nobody would have thought that we had a mind'.
Richard Rorty[3]

'The taste of the apple [. . .] lies in the contact of the fruit with the palate, not in the fruit itself; in a similar way [. . .] poetry lies in the meeting of poem and reader, not in the lines of symbols printed on the pages of a book. What is essential is the aesthetic act, the thrill, the almost physical emotion that comes with each reading'.
Jorge Luis Borges[4]

'How would the painter or poet express anything other than his encounter with the world?'
Maurice Merleau-Ponty[5]

Vision and Knowledge

In Western culture, sight has historically been regarded as the most important and noble of the senses, and thinking and understanding are thought of in terms of seeing. Already in classical Greek thought, certainty was based on vision and visibility. 'The eyes are more exact witnesses than the ears', wrote Heraclitus in one of his fragments.[6] Plato regarded vision as humanity's greatest gift,[7] and he insisted that ethical universals must be accessible to 'the mind's eye'.[8] Aristotle, likewise, considered sight as the most noble of the senses 'because it approximates the intellect most closely by virtue of the relative immateriality of its knowing'.[9]

Since the Greeks, philosophical writings of all times have abounded with ocular metaphors to the point that knowledge has become analogous with clear vision, and light is regarded as the metaphor for truth. Aquinas even applies the notion of sight to other sensory realms as well as to intellectual cognition.

The impact of the sense of vision on philosophy is well summed up by Peter Sloterdijk: 'The eyes are the organic prototype of philosophy. Their enigma is that they not only can see but are also able to see themselves seeing. This gives them a prominence among the body's cognitive organs. A good part of philosophical thinking is actually only eye reflex, eye dialectic, seeing-oneself-see'.[10] During the Renaissance, the five senses were understood to form a hierarchical system from the highest sense of vision down to touch; this had already been the hierarchy of the senses in Aristotle's thinking. The Renaissance system of the senses was related to the image of the cosmic body; vision was correlated to fire and light, hearing to air, smell to vapour, taste to water and touch to earth.[11]

The invention of perspectival representation by architect Philippo Brunellesci made the eye the centre point of the perceptual world as well as of the concept of the self. Perspectival representation itself turned into a symbolic form, one which not only describes but also conditions perception.

There is no doubt that our technological culture has ordered and separated the senses even more distinctly. Vision and hearing are now the privileged sociable senses, whereas the other three are considered as archaic sensory remnants with a merely private function, and they are usually suppressed by the code of culture. Only sensations such as the olfactory enjoyment of a meal, fragrance of flowers and responses to temperature are allowed to draw collective awareness in our ocularcentric and obsessively hygienic code of culture.

The dominance of vision over the other senses – and the consequent bias in cognition – has been observed by many philosophers. A collection of philosophical essays entitled *Modernity and the Hegemony of Vision*, edited by David Michael Lewin, argues that 'beginning with the ancient Greeks, Western culture has been dominated by an ocularcentric paradigm, a vision-generated, vision-centred interpretation of knowledge, truth, and reality'.[12] This thought-provoking book analyses 'historical connections between vision and knowledge, vision and ontology, vision and power, vision and ethics'.[13]

As the ocularcentric paradigm of our relation to the world and of our concept of knowledge – the epistemological privileging of vision – has been revealed by philosophers, it is also important to survey critically the role of vision in relation to the other senses in our understanding and practice of the art of architecture. Architecture, as with all art, is fundamentally confronted with questions of human existence in space and time; it expresses and relates man's being in the world. Architecture is deeply engaged in the metaphysical questions of the self and the world, interiority and exteriority, time and duration and life and death. 'Aesthetic and cultural practices are peculiarly susceptible to the changing experience of space and time precisely because they entail the construction of spatial representations and artefacts out of the flow of human experience', writes David Harvey.[14] Architecture is our primary instrument for relating us with space and time and giving these dimensions a human measure and meaning. It domesticates limitless and shapeless space and endless time to be experienced, inhabited and understood by humankind. Architecture turns nameless and meaningless physical space into experiential and habitable places, the human domicile. We do not live in abstract space; we exist in nameable places and related situations. We become part of the place, and it becomes part of us, while space is doomed to remain as a conceptual abstraction. As a consequence of this interdependence of place, space and time, the dialectics of external and internal space, physical and spiritual, material and mental and unconscious and conscious priorities concerning the senses as well as their relative roles and interactions, have an essential impact on the nature of the arts and architecture. Architecture is fundamentally an art of relatedness.

David Michael Levin motivates the philosophical critique of the dominance of the eye with the following words: 'I think it is appropriate to challenge the hegemony of vision – the ocularcentrism of our culture. And I think we need to examine very critically the character of vision that predominates today in our world.

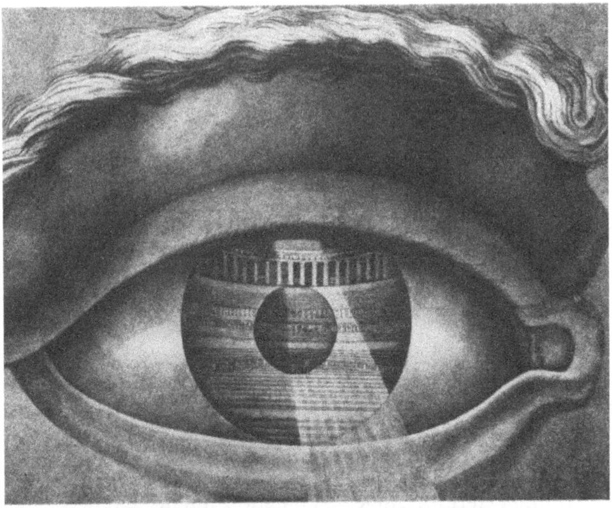

1

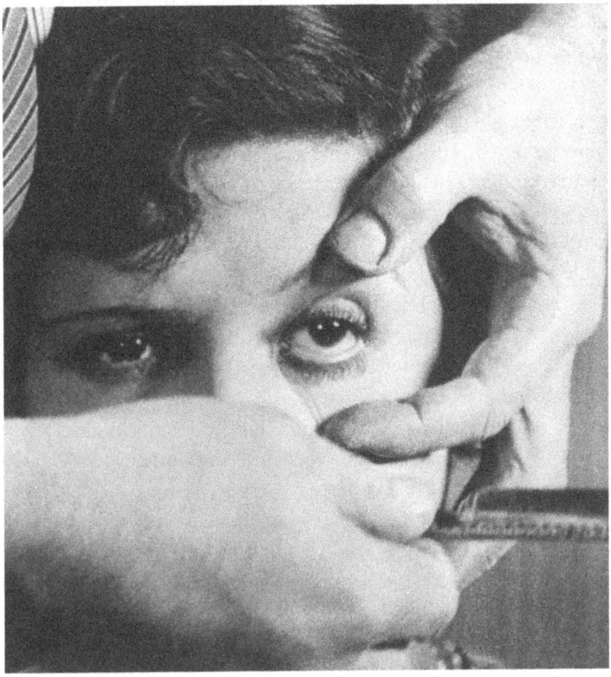

2

OCULARCENTRISM AND THE VIOLATION OF THE EYE

1 Architecture has been regarded as an art form of the eye.

Eye Reflecting the Interior of the Theatre of Besançon (detail), engraving after Claude-Nicolas Ledoux. The theatre was built from 1775 to 1784.

2 Vision is regarded as the most noble of the senses, and the loss of eyesight as the ultimate physical loss.

Luis Buñuel and Salvador Dalí, *Un Chien Andalou (Andalusian Dog)*, 1929. The shocking scene in which the heroine's eye is sliced with a razor blade.

We urgently need a diagnosis of the psychosocial pathologies of everyday seeing – and a critical understanding of ourselves, as visionary beings'.[15] It is also essential to understand how we have been and increasingly are extending our senses through technological devices and, on the other hand, how these technological extensions alter our natural senses developed by processes of timeless evolution. Our technological inventions also change our ways of thinking, understanding and feeling, and these changes even have ethical consequences.

Levin points out the autonomy drive and aggressiveness of vision, and 'the specters of patriarchal rule' that haunt our ocularcentric culture:

> The will to power is very strong in vision. There is a very strong tendency in vision to grasp and fixate, to reify and totalise: a tendency to dominate, secure, and control, which eventually, because it was so extensively promoted, assumed a certain uncontested hegemony over our culture and its philosophical discourse, establishing, in keeping with the instrumental rationality of our culture and the technological character of our society, an ocularcentric metaphysics of presence.[16]

I believe that many aspects of the pathology of everyday architecture today can likewise be understood through an analysis of the epistemology of the senses and a critique of the ocular bias of our culture at large, and of architecture in particular. The inhumanity of contemporary architecture and cities can be understood as the consequence of the neglect of the body and the senses and an imbalance in our sensory and value system. The growing experiences of alienation, detachment and solitude in the technological world today, for instance, may be related to a certain obsessive orientation in today's technologies. It is thought-provoking that this sense of estrangement and detachment is often evoked most clearly by the technologically most advanced settings, such as hospitals and airports. The dominance of the eye and the suppression of the other senses tend to push us into detachment, isolation and outsideness. The art of the eye has certainly produced imposing, thought-provoking and poetic structures and images, but it has not facilitated human rootedness in the world. The fact that the Modernist idiom has not generally been able to penetrate the surface of popular taste and values seems to be due to its one-sided intellectual and visual emphasis; Modernist design at large has housed the intellect and the eye, but it has left the body and the other senses, as well as our memories, imagination and dreams, homeless.

Critics of Ocularcentrism

The ocularcentric tradition and the consequent spectator theory of knowledge in Western thinking already had their critics among philosophers before today's concerns. René Descartes, for instance, regarded vision as the most universal and noble of the senses, and his objectifying philosophy is consequently grounded in the privileging of vision. However, he also equated vision with touch, a sense which he considered to be 'more certain and less vulnerable to error than vision'.[17]

Friedrich Nietzsche attempted to subvert the authority of ocular thinking in seeming contradiction with the general line of his thought. He criticised the 'eye outside of time and history'[18] presumed by many philosophers. He even accused philosophers of a 'treacherous and blind hostility towards the senses'.[19] Max Scheler bluntly calls this attitude the 'hatred of the body'.[20]

The forcefully critical 'anti-ocularcentric' view of Western ocularcentric perception and thinking, which developed in the 20th-century French intellectual tradition, is thoroughly surveyed by Martin Jay in his book *Downcast Eyes: The Denigration of Vision in Twentieth-Century French Thought*.[21] The writer traces the development of the modern vision-centred culture through such diverse fields as the invention of the printing press, artificial illumination, photography, visual poetry and the new experience of time. On the other hand, he analyses the anti-ocular positions of many of the seminal French writers, such as Henri Bergson, Georges Bataille, Jean-Paul Sartre, Maurice Merleau-Ponty, Jacques Lacan, Louis Althusser, Guy Debord, Roland Barthes, Jacques Derrida, Luce Irigaray, Emmanuel Levinas and Jean-François Lyotard.

Sartre was outspokenly hostile to the sense of vision to the point of ocularphobia; his oeuvre has been estimated to contain 7000 references to 'the look'.[22] He was concerned with 'the objectifying look of the other, and the "medusa glance" [which] "petrifies" everything that it comes in contact with'.[23] In his view, space has taken over time in human consciousness as a consequence of ocularcentrism.[24] This change is also clear in the development of Western literature, which was dominated by the dimension of time, but became engaged primarily in issues of space around the beginning of the 20th century. This reversal of the relative significance accorded to the notions of space and time has important repercussions on our understanding of physical and historical processes. The prevailing concepts of space and time and their interrelations form an essential paradigm for architecture, as Sigfried Giedion established in his seminal ideological history of modern architecture, *Space, Time and Architecture*.[25] Giedion quotes the mathematician Hermann Minkowsky's credo: 'Henceforth, space alone or time alone is doomed to fade into a mere shadow: only a kind of union of both will preserve their existence'.[26] This view surely applies in physics, but not in the experiential art of architecture, which is grounded in our sensory, mental and experiential realities. Simply, architecture is not a scientific practise, it is an art of human existential mediation, which includes numerous aspects of science.

Maurice Merleau-Ponty launched a ceaseless critique of the 'Cartesian perspectivalist scopic regime' and 'its privileging of an ahistorical, disinterested, disembodied subject entirely outside of the world'.[27] His entire philosophical work focuses on perception in general, and vision in particular. But instead of the Cartesian eye of the outside spectator, Merleau-Ponty's sense of sight is an embodied vision that is an incarnate part of the 'flesh of the world':[28] 'Our body is both an object among objects and that which sees and touches them'.[29] The philosopher saw an osmotic relation between the self and the world – they interpenetrate and mutually define each other – and he emphasised the simultaneity and interaction of the senses. 'My perception is [therefore] not a sum of visual, tactile and audible givens: I perceive in a total way with my whole being: I grasp a unique structure of the thing, a unique way of being, which speaks to all my senses at once', he writes.[30]

Martin Heidegger, Michel Foucault and Jacques Derrida have all argued that the thought and culture of modernity have not only continued the historical privileging of sight but furthered its negative tendencies. Each, in their own separate ways, has regarded the sight-dominance of the modern era as distinctly different from that of earlier times. The hegemony of vision has been reinforced in our time by a multitude of technological inventions and the endless multiplication and production of images – 'an unending rainfall of images', as Italo Calvino calls it.[31] 'The fundamental event of the modern age is the conquest of the world as picture', writes Heidegger.[32] The philosopher's speculation has certainly materialised in our age of the fabricated, mass-produced and manipulated image.

The technologically expanded and strengthened eye today penetrates deep into matter and space and enables man to cast a simultaneous look on the opposite sides of the globe. The experiences of space and time have become fused into each other by speed (David Harvey uses the notion of 'time–space compression'[33]), and as a consequence, we are witnessing a distinct reversal of the two dimensions – a temporalisation of space and a spatialisation of time. The only sense that is fast enough to keep pace with the astounding increase of speed in the technological world is sight. But the world of the eye is causing us to live increasingly in a perpetual present, flattened by speed, lack of depth and simultaneity. Visual images have become commodities, as Harvey points out: 'A rush of images from different spaces almost simultaneously, collapsing the world's spaces into a series of images on a television screen [. . .] The image of places and spaces become as open to production and ephemeral use as any other [commodity]'.[34]

The dramatic shattering of the inherited experiential construction of reality in recent decades has undoubtedly resulted in a crisis of identity and representation. We can even identify a certain panicked hysteria of representation in the arts of our time.

The Narcissistic and Nihilistic Eye

The hegemony of sight first brought forth glorious visions, in Heidegger's view, but it has turned increasingly nihilistic in modern times. Heidegger's observation of a nihilistic eye is particularly thought-provoking today; many of the architectural projects of the past 20 years, celebrated by the international architectural press, express both narcissism and nihilism.

The hegemonic eye seeks domination over all fields of cultural production, and it seems to weaken our capacity for empathy, compassion and participation with the world. The narcissistic eye views architecture solely as a means of self-expression and as an intellectual–artistic game detached from essential mental and societal connections and meanings, whereas the nihilistic eye deliberately advances sensory and mental detachment and alienation. Instead of reinforcing one's body-centred and integrated experience of the world, nihilistic architecture disengages and isolates the body, and instead of attempting to reconstruct cultural order, it makes a reading of collective signification impossible. The world becomes a hedonistic but meaningless visual journey. It is clear that only the distancing and detaching sense of vision is capable of a nihilistic attitude; it is impossible to think of a nihilistic sense of touch, for instance, because of the unavoidable nearness, intimacy, veracity and identification that the sense of touch carries. A sadistic as well as a masochistic eye also exists, and their instruments in the fields of contemporary arts and architecture can also be identified.

The current industrial mass production of visual imagery tends to alienate vision from emotional involvement and identification and turn imagery into a mesmerising flow without focus or participation. Michel de Certeau perceives the expansion of the ocular realm negatively indeed: 'From television to newspapers, from advertising to all sorts of mercantile epiphanies, our society is characterised by a cancerous growth of vision, measuring everything by its ability to show or be shown, and transmuting communication into a visual journey'.[35] The cancerous spread of superficial architectural imagery today, devoid of tectonic logic and a sense of materiality and empathy, is clearly part of this process.

Oral Versus Visual Space

But man has not always been dominated by vision. In fact, a primordial dominance of hearing has only gradually been replaced by that of vision. Anthropological literature describes numerous cultures in which our private senses of smell, taste and touch continue to have collective importance in behaviour and communication. The roles of the senses in the utilisation of collective and personal space in various cultures were the subject matter of Edward T Hall's seminal book *The Hidden Dimension*, which, regrettably, seems to have been forgotten by architects.[36] Hall's proxemic studies of personal space offer important insights into instinctual and unconscious aspects of our relation to space and our unconscious use of space in behavioural communication. Hall's insights can serve as the basis for the design of intimate, bio-culturally functional and meaningful spaces.

Walter J Ong analyses the transition from oral to written culture and its impact on human consciousness and the sense of the collective in his book *Orality and Literacy*.[37] He points out that 'the shift from oral to written speech was essentially a shift from sound to visual space',[38] and that 'print replaced the lingering hearing-dominance in the world of thought and expression with the sight-dominance which had its beginning in writing'.[39] In Ong's view, '[t]his is an insistent world of cold, non-human facts'.[40]

Ong analyses the changes that the shift from the primordial oral culture to the culture of the written (and eventually the printed) word has caused in

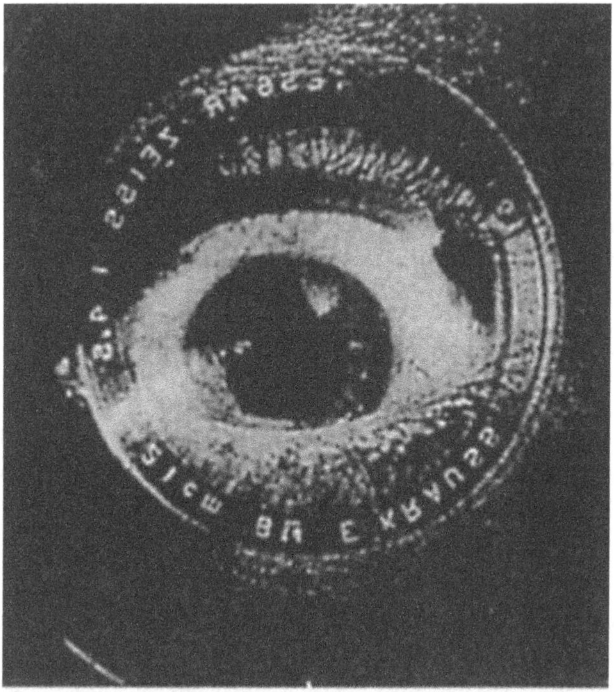

3

4

THE POWER AND THE WEAKNESS OF THE EYE

3 Particularly in modern times, vision has been strengthened by numerous technological inventions. We are now able to see deep into both the secrets of matter and the immensities of outer space.

The eye of the camera, detail from the film *The Man with a Movie Camera* by Dziga Vertov, 1929.

4 Regardless of our prioritisation of the eye, visual observation is often confirmed by our touch.

Caravaggio, *The Incredulity of Saint Thomas* (detail), 1601–2, Sanssouci Picture Gallery, Potsdam.

---

human consciousness, memory and understanding of space. He argues that as hearing-dominance has yielded to sight-dominance, situational thinking has been replaced by abstract thinking. This fundamental change in the perception and understanding of the world seems irreversible to the writer: 'Though words are grounded in oral speech, writing tyrannically locks them into a visual field forever [. . .] a literate person cannot fully recover a sense of what the word is to purely oral people'.[41]

In fact, the unchallenged hegemony of the eye may be a fairly recent phenomenon regardless of its origins in Greek thought and optics. In Lucien Febvre's view: 'The sixteenth century did not see first: it heard and smelled, it sniffed the air and caught sounds. It was only later that it seriously and actively became engaged in geometry, focusing attention on the world of forms with Kepler (1571–1630) and Desargues of Lyon (1593–1662). It was then that vision was unleashed in the world of science as it was in the world of physical sensations, and the world of beauty as well'.[42] Robert Mandrou makes a parallel argument: 'The hierarchy [of the senses] was not the same [as in the twentieth century] because the eye, which rules today, found itself in third place, behind hearing and touch, and far after them. The eye that organises, classifies and orders was not the favoured organ of a time that preferred hearing'.[43]

The gradually growing hegemony of the eye seems to be parallel with the development of Western ego-consciousness and the gradually increasing separation of the self and the world; vision separates us from the world, whereas the other senses unite us with it.

Artistic expression is engaged with pre-verbal meanings of the world, meanings that are incorporated and lived rather than simply intellectually understood. In my view, poetry has the capacity to bring us momentarily back to the oral and enveloping world. The re-oralised word of poetry brings us back to the centre of an interior world. The poet speaks not only 'on the threshold of being', as Gaston Bachelard notes,[44] but also on the threshold of language. Equally, the task of art and architecture in general is to reconstruct the experience of an undifferentiated interior world, in which we are not mere spectators, but to which we inseparably belong. In artistic works, existential understanding arises from our very encounter with the world and our being-in-the-world – it is not conceptualised or intellectualised.

Retinal Architecture and the Loss of Plasticity

It is evident that the architecture of traditional cultures is also essentially connected with the tacit wisdom of the body, instead of being visually and conceptually structured and dominated. Construction in traditional cultures is guided by the body – not only the individual body but also the societal and cultural bodies – in the same way that a bird shapes its nest by movements of its body. Indigenous clay and mud architectures in various parts of the world seem to be born of the muscular and haptic senses more than the eye. We can even identify the transition of indigenous construction from the haptic realm into the control of vision as a loss of plasticity and intimacy and of the sense of total fusion characteristic in the settings of indigenous cultures.

The dominance of the sense of vision pointed out in philosophical thought is equally evident in the development of Western architecture. Greek architecture, with its elaborate systems of optical corrections, was already ultimately refined for the pleasure of the eye. However, the privileging of sight does not necessarily imply a rejection of the other senses, as the haptic sensibility, materiality and authoritative weight of Greek architecture prove; the eye invites and stimulates muscular and tactile sensations. The sense of sight may incorporate, and even reinforce, other sense modalities; the unconscious tactile ingredient in vision is particularly important and strongly present in historical architecture, but badly neglected in the architecture of our time.

Western architectural theory since Leon Battista Alberti has been primarily engaged with questions of visual perception, harmony and proportion. Alberti's statement that 'painting is nothing but the intersection of the visual pyramid following a given distance, a fixed centre and a certain lighting' outlines the perspectival paradigm, which also became the instrument of architectural thinking.[45] Again, it has to be emphasised that the conscious focusing on the mechanics of vision did not automatically result in the decisive and deliberate rejection of other senses before our own era of the omnipresent manipulating visual image. The eye conquers its hegemonic role in architectural practice, both consciously and unconsciously, only gradually with the emergence of the idea of a bodiless observer. The observer becomes detached from an incarnate and existential relation with the environment through the suppression of the other senses, in particular by means of technological extensions of the eye, and the proliferation of images. As Marx W Wartofsky argues, 'the human vision is itself an artifact, produced by other artifacts, namely pictures'.[46]

The dominant sense of vision figures strongly in the writings of the Modernists. Statements by Le Corbusier – such as: 'I exist in life only if I can see';[47] 'I am and I remain an impenitent visual – everything is in the visual';[48] 'One needs to see clearly in order to understand';[49] 'I urge you to *open your eyes*. Do you open your eyes? Are you trained to open your eyes? Do you know how to open your eyes, do you open them often, always, well?';[50] 'Man looks at the creation of architecture with his eyes, which are 5 feet 6 inches from the ground'[51] and, 'Architecture is a plastic thing. I mean by "plastic" what is seen and measured by the eyes'[52] – make the privileging of the eye in early Modernist theory very clear. Further declarations by Walter Gropius – 'He [the designer] has to adapt knowledge of the scientific facts of optics and thus obtain a theoretical ground that will guide the hand giving shape, and create an objective basis'[53] and by László Moholy-Nagy: 'The hygiene of the optical, the health of the visible is slowly filtering through'[54] – confirm the central role of vision in Modernist thought.

Le Corbusier's famous credo, 'Architecture is the masterly, correct and magnificent play of masses brought together in light',[55] unquestionably defines an architecture of the eye. Le Corbusier, however, was a great artistic talent with a moulding hand and a tremendous sense of materiality, plasticity and gravity, all of which prevented his architecture from turning into sensory reductivism. Regardless of Le Corbusier's Cartesian ocularcentric exclamations, the hand had a similar fetishistic role in his work as the eye. A vigorous element of tactility is present in Le Corbusier's sketches and paintings, and this haptic sensibility is incorporated into his regard for architecture. However, the reductive bias becomes devastating in his urbanistic projects and the uncritical acceptance of his theorizing.

5

6

THE SUPPRESSION OF VISION – THE FUSION OF VISION AND TACTILITY

5 In heightened emotional states and deep thought, vision is usually repressed.

René Magritte, *The Lovers* (detail), 1928, Museum of Modern Art, New York (gift of Richard S Zeisler).

6 Vision and the tactile sense are fused in actual lived experience.

Herbert Bayer, *Lonely Metropolitan*, 1932 (detail), Buhl Collection.

In Mies van der Rohe's architecture, a frontal perspectival perception predominates, but his unique sense of order, structure, weight, detail and craft decisively enriches the visual paradigm. Moreover, an architectural work is great precisely because of the oppositional and contradictory intentions and allusions it succeeds in fusing together. A tension between conscious intentions and unconscious drives is necessary for a work in order to open up the emotional participation of the observer. 'In every case one must achieve a simultaneous solution of opposites', as Alvar Aalto wrote.[56] The verbal statements of artists and architects should not usually be taken at their face value, as they often merely represent a conscious surface rationalisation, or an intellectualized defence, that may well be in sharp contradiction with the deeper unconscious intentions giving the work its very life force.

With equal clarity, the visual paradigm is the prevailing condition in city planning, from the idealised town plans of the Renaissance to the Functionalist principles of zoning and planning that reflect the 'hygiene of the optical'. In particular, the contemporary city is increasingly the city of the eye, detached from the body by rapid motorised movement, or through the overall aerial grasp from an aeroplane. The processes of planning have favoured the idealising and disembodied Cartesian eye of control and detachment; city plans are highly idealised and schematised visions seen through *le regard surplombant* (the look from above), as defined by Jean Starobinski,[57] or through 'the mind's eye' of Plato.

Until recently, architectural theory and criticism have been almost exclusively engaged with the mechanisms of vision and visual expression. The perception and experience of architectural form has most frequently been analysed through the Gestalt laws of visual perception. Educational philosophy has likewise understood architecture primarily in terms of vision, emphasising the construction of three-dimensional visual images in space.

An Architecture of Visual Images

The ocular bias has never been more apparent in the art of architecture than in the past half century, as a type of architecture, aimed at a striking and memorable visual image, has predominated. Instead of an existentially grounded plastic and spatial experience, architecture has adopted the psychological strategy of advertising and instant persuasion; buildings have turned into image products detached from existential depth, veracity and sincerity. Instead of mediating and fusing the multitude of aspects of the environments, the architecture of the modern era has tended to separate and isolate. Instead of aspiring for harmony, contrasts have been sought.

David Harvey relates 'the loss of temporality and the search for instantaneous impact' in contemporary expression to the loss of experiential depth.[58] Fredric Jameson uses the notion of 'contrived depthlessness' to describe the contemporary cultural condition and 'its fixation with appearances, surfaces and instant impacts that have no sustaining power over time'.[59] The experiential depth arises from the fusion of conscious, focused vision and unconscious, unfocused peripheral expressions, as well as the dialogue between the work and the world.

Artistic and architectural meaning is always relational and mediating. It expresses our relation with the world rather than itself. Maurice Merleau-Ponty expresses this fundamental relatedness of art succinctly: 'We come to see not the work of art, but the world according to the work'.[60]

As a consequence of the current deluge of images, architecture of our time most often appears as mere retinal art, thus completing an epistemological cycle that began in Greek thought and architecture. But the change goes beyond mere visual dominance; instead of being a situational bodily encounter, architecture has become an art of the printed image fixed by the hurried eye of the camera. In our culture of pictures, the gaze itself flattens into a picture and loses its plasticity. Instead of experiencing our being in the world, we behold it from outside as spectators of images projected on the surface of the retina. David Michael Levin uses the term 'frontal ontology' to describe the prevailing frontal, fixated and focused vision.[61]

Susan Sontag has made perceptive remarks on the role of the photographed image in our perception of the world. She writes, for instance, of a 'mentality which looks at the world as a set of potential photographs',[62] and argues that 'the reality has come to seem more and more what we are shown by camera',[63] and that 'the omnipresence of photographs has an incalculable effect on our ethical sensibility. By furnishing this already crowded world with a duplicate one of images, photography makes us feel that the world is more available than it really is'.[64]

As buildings lose their plasticity and their connection with the language and wisdom of the body, they become isolated in the cool and distant realm of vision. With the loss of tactility, measures and details crafted for the human body – and particularly for the hand – architectural structures become repulsively flat, sharp-edged, immaterial and unreal. The detachment of construction from the realities of matter and craft further turns architecture into stage sets for the eye, into a scenography devoid of the authenticity of matter and construction. The sense of 'aura', the authority of presence, that Walter Benjamin regards as a necessary quality for an authentic piece of art, has been lost. These products of instrumentalised technology conceal their processes of construction, appearing as ghostlike apparitions. The increasing use of reflective glass in architecture reinforces the dreamlike sense of unreality and alienation. The contradictory, opaque transparency of these buildings reflects the gaze back unaffected and unmoved; we are unable to see or imagine life behind these absent walls. The architectural mirror, that returns our gaze and doubles the world, is an enigmatic and frightening device.

Materiality and Time

The flatness of today's standard construction is strengthened by a weakened sense of materiality. Natural materials – stone, brick and wood – allow our vision to penetrate their surfaces and enable us to become convinced of the veracity of matter. Natural materials express their age, as well as the story of their biological origins and their history of human manufacture and timeless use. All matter exists in the continuum of time; the patina of wear adds the enriching experience of time to the materials of construction. But the machine-made materials of today – scaleless sheets of glass, enamelled metals and synthetic plastics – tend to present their unyielding surfaces to the eye without conveying their material essence or age. Buildings of this technological era usually deliberately aim at ageless perfection, and they do not incorporate the dimension of time, or the unavoidable and mentally significant processes of ageing. This fear of the traces of wear and age is surely related to our unconscious uneasiness with or fear of death. The relation of our culture 'of reason' to death is becoming increasingly problematic in comparison to traditional societies whose relation to the unavoidability of decay and death was less problematic.

Transparency and sensations of weightlessness and flotation are central themes in modern art and architecture. In recent decades, a new architectural imagery has emerged, which employs reflection, gradations of transparency, overlay and juxtaposition to create a sense of spatial thickness, as well as subtle and changing sensations of movement and light. This new sensibility promises an architecture that can turn the relative immateriality and weightlessness of recent technological construction into a positive experience of place and meaning. The weakening of the experience of time in today's environments has devastating mental effects. In the words of the American therapist Gotthard Booth, 'nothing gives man fuller satisfaction than participation in processes that supersede the span of individual life'.[65] We have a mental need to grasp that we are rooted in the continuity of time, and in the man-made world it is the task of architecture to facilitate this temporal experience. Architecture domesticates and names limitless space and enables us to inhabit it, but it should likewise domesticate endless time and enable us to inhabit the continuum of time. The earliest human construction was not a construction, but a recognition and marking of a place, and, much later, naming a place; by marking and naming we take possession of things.

The current overemphasis on the intellectual and conceptual dimensions of architecture contributes to the disappearance of its physical, sensual and embodied essences. Contemporary architecture posing as the avant-garde is more often engaged with the architectural discourse itself and mapping the possible marginal territories of the art than with responding to genuine human existential questions. This reductive focus gives rise to a sense of architectural autism, an internalised and autonomous discourse that is not grounded in our shared existential reality and desire.

Beyond architecture, contemporary culture at large drifts towards a distancing, a kind of chilling de-sensualisation and de-eroticisation of the human relation to reality. Painting and sculpture also seem to be losing their sensuality; instead of inviting a sensory intimacy, contemporary works of art frequently signal a distancing rejection of sensuous curiosity and pleasure. These works speak to the intellect and to the conceptualising capacities instead of addressing the senses and the undifferentiated embodied responses. The ceaseless bombardment of unrelated imagery leads to a gradual emptying of images of their emotional content. Images are converted into endless commodities manufactured to postpone boredom; humans in turn are commodified, consuming themselves nonchalantly without having the courage or even the possibility of confronting their very existential reality. We are now made to live in fabricated dream worlds.

I do not wish to express a conservative view of contemporary art in the tone of Hans Sedlmayr's thought-provoking but disturbing book *Art in Crisis*.[66] I merely suggest that a distinct change has occurred in our sensory and perceptual

---

THE CITY OF THE EYE – THE HAPTIC CITY

7 The contemporary city is the city of the eye, one of distance and exteriority.

Le Corbusier's proposed skyline for Buenos Aires – a sketch from a lecture given in Buenos Aires in 1929.

8 The haptic city is the city of interiority and nearness.

The hill town of Casares, southern Spain.
Photo: Juhani Pallasmaa

7 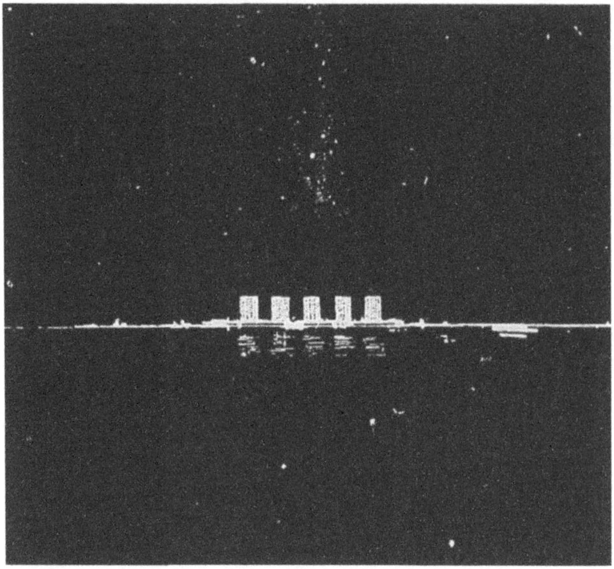

8 

experience of the world, one that is reflected in art and architecture. If we desire architecture to have an emancipating or healing role, instead of reinforcing the erosion of existential meaning, we must reflect on the multitude of secret ways in which the art of architecture is tied to the cultural and mental reality of its time. We should also be aware of the ways in which the feasibility of architecture is being threatened or marginalised by current political, cultural, economic, cognitive and perceptual developments. Architecture has become an endangered art form.

The Rejection of Alberti's Window

The eye itself has not, of course, remained in the monocular, fixed construction defined by Renaissance theories of perspective. The hegemonic eye has conquered new ground for visual perception and expression. The paintings of Hieronymus Bosch and Pieter Bruegel, for instance, invite a participatory eye to travel across the scenes of multiple events. The 17th-century Dutch paintings of bourgeois life present casual scenes and objects of everyday use which expand beyond the boundaries of the Albertian window. Baroque paintings open up vision with hazy edges, soft focus and multiple perspectives, presenting a distinct, tactile invitation and enticing the body to travel through the illusory space.

An essential line in the evolution of modernity has been the liberation of the eye from the Cartesian perspectival epistemology. The paintings of

---

ARCHITECTURE AND THE HUMAN FIGURE

9 We tend to interpret a building as an analogue to our body, and vice versa.

Caryatids of the Erechtheum on the Acropolis of Athens (421–405 BC), British Museum, London.

10 Since the dynasties of ancient Egypt, measures of the human body have been used in architecture. The anthropocentric tradition has been almost entirely forgotten in modern times.

Aulis Blomstedt's study of a proportional system for architecture based on the Pythagorean subdivision of a basic 180 cm measure (presumably from the early 1960s).

9

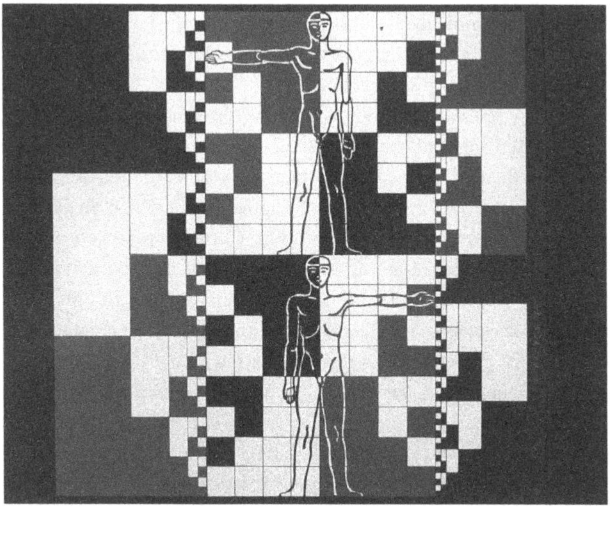

10

Joseph Mallord William Turner continue the elimination of the picture frame and the vantage point begun in the Baroque era; the Impressionists abandon the boundary line, balanced framing and perspectival depth; Paul Cézanne aspires 'to make visible how the world touches us';[67] Cubists abandon the single focal point, reactivate peripheral vision and reinforce haptic experience, whereas the colour field painters reject illusory depth in order to reinforce the presence of the painting itself as an iconic artefact and an autonomous reality. Land artists fuse the reality of the work with the reality of the lived world, and finally, artists such as Richard Serra directly address the body as well as our experiences of horizontality and verticality, materiality, gravity and weight.

The same countercurrent against the hegemony of the perspectival eye has taken place in modern architecture regardless of the culturally privileged position of vision. The kinaesthetic and textural architecture of Frank Lloyd Wright, the muscular and tactile buildings of Alvar Aalto and Louis Kahn's architecture of geometry and gravitas are particularly significant examples of this.

A New Vision and Sensory Balance

Perhaps, freed of the implicit desire of the eye for control and power, it is precisely the unfocused vision of our time that is again capable of opening up new realms of vision and thought. The loss of focus brought about by the stream of images may emancipate the eye from its patriarchal domination and give rise to a participatory and empathetic gaze. The technological extensions of the senses have until now reinforced the primacy of vision, but the new technologies may also help 'the body [. . .] to dethrone the disinterested gaze of the disincarnated Cartesian spectator'.[68]

Martin Jay remarks: 'In opposition to the lucid, linear, solid, fixed, planimetric, closed form of the Renaissance [. . .] the baroque was painterly, recessional, soft-focused, multiple, and open'.[69] He also argues that the 'baroque visual experience has a strongly tactile or haptic quality, which prevents it from turning into the absolute ocularcentrism of its Cartesian perspectivalist rival'.[70]

The haptic experience seems to be penetrating the ocular regime again through the tactile presence of modern visual imagery. In a music video, for instance, or the layered contemporary urban transparency, we cannot halt the flow of images for analytic observation; instead, we have to appreciate it as an enhanced haptic sensation, rather like a swimmer senses the flow of water against his/her skin.

In his thorough and thought-provoking book *The Opening of Vision: Nihilism and the Postmodern Situation*, David Michael Levin differentiates between two modes of vision: 'the assertoric gaze' and 'the aletheic gaze'.[71] In his view, the assertoric gaze is narrow, dogmatic, intolerant, rigid, fixed, inflexible, exclusionary and unmoved, whereas the aletheic gaze, associated with the hermeneutic theory of truth, tends to see from a multiplicity of standpoints and perspectives, and is multiple, pluralistic, democratic, contextual, inclusionary, horizontal and caring.[72] As suggested by Levin, there are signs that a new mode of looking is emerging.

Although the new technologies have strengthened the hegemony of vision, they may also help to re-balance the realms of the senses. In Walter Ong's view, 'with telephone, radio, television and various kinds of sound tape, electronic technology has brought us into the age of "secondary orality". This new orality has striking resemblances to the old in its participatory mystique, its fostering of communal sense, its concentration on the present moment [. . .]'.[73]

'We in the Western world are beginning to discover our neglected senses. This growing awareness represents something of an overdue insurgency against the painful deprivation of sensory experience we have suffered in our technologised world', writes the anthropologist Ashley Montagu.[74] This new awareness is forcefully projected by numerous architects around the world today who are attempting to re-sensualise architecture through a strengthened sense of materiality and hapticity, texture and weight, density of space and materialised light.

PART *TWO*

As the preceding brief survey suggests, the privileging of the sense of sight over the other senses is an inarguable theme in Western thought, and it has also turned into an evident bias in the theory, thinking and practice of architecture in the modern era. This negative development in architecture is, of course, forcefully supported by forces and patterns of management, organisation, production and economic system, as well as by the abstracting and universalising impact of technological rationality and value system itself. The negative developments in the realm of the senses cannot, either, be directly attributed to the historical privileging of the sense of vision itself. The understanding of sight as our most important sense is well grounded in physiological, perceptual and psychological facts.[75] The problems arise from the isolation of the eye outside its natural and biological interaction with the other sense modalities and from the unconscious elimination and suppression of other senses, which increasingly reduce and restrict the experience of the world into the sphere of vision. This separation and reduction fragments the innate complexity, comprehensiveness and plasticity of the perceptual system, reinforcing the experience of a sense of detachment and alienation, 'the existential outsideness', to use the expression of Edward Relph in *Place and Placelessness*.[76]

In this second part, I will survey the interactions of the senses and give some personal impressions of the realms of the senses in the expression and experience of architecture. In this essay, I proclaim an integrated sensory architecture in opposition to the prevailing visual understanding of the art of building.

The Body in the Centre

I confront the city with my body; my legs measure the length of the arcade and the width of the square; my gaze unconsciously projects my body onto the facade of the cathedral, where it roams over the mouldings and contours, sensing the size of recesses and projections; my body weight meets the mass of the cathedral door, and my hand grasps the door pull as I enter the silent dark void behind. I experience myself in the city, and the city exists through my embodied experience. The city and my body supplement and define each other. I dwell in the city, and the city dwells in me. Architecture is the artform of perpetual relatedness and exchange. John Dewey suggested that the human mind is a verb;[77] I suggest that architecture is also a verb instead of a noun.

Merleau-Ponty's philosophy makes the human body the centre of the experiential world. He consistently argued, as Richard Kearney summarises, that '[i]t is through our bodies as living centres of intentionality [. . .] that we choose our world and that our world chooses us'.[78] In Merleau-Ponty's own words, 'Our own body is in the world as the heart is in the organism: it keeps the visible spectacle constantly alive, it breathes life into it and sustains it inwardly, and with it forms a system';[79] and '[s]ensory experience is unstable and alien to natural perception, which we achieve with our whole body all at once, and which opens on a world of interacting senses'.[80]

Sensory experiences become integrated through the body, or rather, in the very constitution of the body and the human mode of being. Psychoanalytic theory has introduced the notion of body image or body schema as the centre of integration. Human existence is a relational and relating mode of being. Our bodies and movements are in constant interaction with the environment; the world and the self inform and redefine each other constantly. The percept of the body and the image of the world turn into one single continuous existential experience of being; there is no body separate from its domicile in place, and there is no space unrelated to the unconscious image of the perceiving self. 'The body image [. . .] is informed fundamentally from haptic and orienting experiences early in life. Our visual images are developed later on, and depend for their meaning on primal experiences that were acquired haptically', Kent C Bloomer and Charles W Moore argue in their 1977 book *Body, Memory, and Architecture*, one of the first serious studies to survey the role of the body and of the senses in architectural experience.[81] They go on to explain: 'What is missing from our dwellings today are the potential transactions between body, imagination, and environment';[82] . . . 'To at least some extent every place can be remembered, partly because it is unique, but partly because it has affected our bodies and generated enough associations to hold it in our personal worlds'.[83]

Multi-Sensory Experience

A walk through a forest is invigorating and healing due to the constant interaction of all sense modalities; Bachelard speaks of 'the polyphony of the senses'.[84] The eye collaborates naturally with the body and the other senses. One's sense of reality and self is strengthened and articulated by this constant interaction. Architecture is essentially an extension of nature into the human-made realm, providing the ground for perception and the horizon for experiencing and understanding the world. It is not an isolated and self-sufficient artefact; it directs our attention and existential experience to wider horizons. Architecture also gives a conceptual and material structure to societal institutions as well as to the conditions of daily life. Even ideas of urbanity and social institutions are administrative abstractions until they become materialised in architecture. It also concretises the cycle of the year, the course of the sun and the passing of the hours of the day.

Every touching experience of architecture is multi-sensory; qualities of place, matter and scale are measured equally by the eye, ear, nose, skin, tongue, skeleton and muscle. Architecture grounds us and strengthens our existential experience, our sense of being in the world, and this is essentially a strengthened experience of self. Instead of mere vision, or the five classical senses, architecture involves several realms of sensory experience which interact and fuse with each other.[85]

The psychologist James J Gibson regards the senses as aggressively seeking mechanisms rather than mere passive receivers. Instead of the five detached senses, Gibson categorises the senses into five sensory systems: the visual system, the auditory system, the taste–smell system, the basic-orienting system and the haptic system.[86] Steinerian philosophy assumes that we actually utilise no fewer than 12 senses.[87] *The Sixth Sense Reader* edited by David Howes even suggests that we have over thirty systems of sensing. We are only beginning to understand the utterly complex functions of our intestinal bacteria in mediating our relationship with our environment; a French scientific television programme called the complexities of our intestinal universe 'our second brain'.

The eyes want to collaborate with the other senses. All the senses, including vision, can be regarded as extensions of the sense of touch – as specialisations of the skin. They define the interface between the skin and the environment – between the opaque interiority of the body and the open exteriority of the world. In the view of René Spitz, 'all perception begins in the oral cavity, which serves as the primeval bridge from inner reception to external perception'.[88] Even the eye touches; the gaze implies an unconscious touch, bodily mimesis and identification.

As Martin Jay remarks when describing Merleau-Ponty's philosophy of the senses, 'through vision we touch the sun and the stars'.[89] Preceding Merleau-Ponty, the 18th-century Irish philosopher and clergyman George Berkeley related touch with vision and assumed that visual apprehension of materiality, distance and spatial depth would not be possible at all without the cooperation of the haptic memory. In Berkeley's view, vision needs the help of touch, which provides sensations of 'solidity, resistance, and protrusion';[90] sight detached from touch could not 'have any idea of distance, outness, or profundity, nor consequently of space or body'.[91] In accord with Berkeley, Hegel claimed that the only sense which can give a sensation of spatial depth is touch, because touch 'senses the weight, resistance, and three-dimensional shape (gestalt) of material bodies, and thus makes us aware that things extend away from us in all directions'.[92]

Vision reveals what the touch already knows. We could think of the sense of touch as the unconscious of vision. Our eyes stroke distant surfaces, contours and edges, and the unconscious tactile sensation determines the agreeableness or unpleasantness of the experience. The distant and the near are experienced with the same intensity, and they merge into one coherent experience. In the words of Merleau-Ponty:

> We see the depth, the smoothness, the softness, the hardness of objects; Cézanne even claimed that we see their odor. If the painter is to express the world, the arrangement of his colors must carry with it this indivisible whole, or else his picture will only hint at things and will not give them in the imperious unity, the presence, the insurpassable plenitude which is for us the definition of the real.[93]

In developing further Goethe's idea that a work of art must be 'life-enhancing',[94] Bernard Berenson suggested that when experiencing an artistic work, we imagine a genuine physical encounter through 'ideated sensations'. The most important of these he called 'tactile values'.[95] In his view, the work of authentic art stimulates our ideated sensations of touch, and this stimulation is life-enhancing. Indeed, we do feel the warmth of the water in the bathtub in Pierre Bonnard's paintings of bathing nudes and the moist air of Turner's landscapes, and we can sense the heat of the sun and the cool breeze in Matisse's paintings of windows open to a view of the sea.

In the same way, an architectural work generates an indivisible complex of impressions. The live encounter with Frank Lloyd Wright's Fallingwater weaves the surrounding forest, the volumes, surfaces, textures and colours of the house, and even the smells of the forest and the sounds of the river, into a uniquely full experience. An architectural work is not experienced as a collection of isolated visual pictures, but in its fully embodied material, existential and spiritual presence. A work of architecture incorporates and infuses both physical and

---

THE CITY OF PARTICIPATION – THE CITY OF ALIENATION

11 The city of sensory engagement.

Pieter Bruegel the Elder, *Children's Games* (detail), 1560, Kunsthistorisches Museum with MVK and ÖTM, Vienna.

12 The modern city of sensory deprivation.

The commercial section of Brasília, Brazil, 1968. Photo: Juhani Pallasmaa

11

12

mental structures. The visual frontality of the architectural drawing is lost in the real experience of architecture. Good architecture offers shapes and surfaces moulded for the pleasurable touch of the eye. 'Contour and profile (*modénature*) are the touchstone of the architect', as Le Corbusier put it, revealing a tactile ingredient in his otherwise ocular understanding of architecture.[96]

Images of one sensory realm feed further imagery in another modality. Images of presence give rise to images of memory, imagination and dream. '[T]he chief benefit of the house [is that] the house shelters daydreaming, the house protects the dreamer, the house allows one to dream in peace', writes Bachelard.[97] But even more, the experience of an architectural space frames, halts, strengthens and focuses our thoughts, and prevents them from getting lost. We can dream and sense our being outdoors, but we need the architectural geometry of a room to think clearly. The geometry of thought echoes the geometry of the room.

In *The Book of Tea*, Kakuzo Okakura gives a subtle description of the multi-sensory imagery evoked by the simple situation of the Japanese tea ceremony:

> Quiet reigns with nothing to break the silence save the note of the boiling water in the iron kettle. The kettle sings well, for pieces of iron are so arranged in the bottom as to produce a peculiar melody in which one may hear the echoes of a cataract muffled by clouds, of a distant sea breaking among the rocks, a rainstorm sweeping through a bamboo forest, or of the soughing of pines on some faraway hill.[98]

In Okakura's description, the present and the absent, the near and the distant and the sensed and the imagined fuse together. The body is not a mere physical entity; it is enriched by both memory and dream, past and future. Edward S Casey even argues that our capacity for memory would be impossible without a body memory.[99] The world is reflected in the body, and the body is projected onto the world. We remember through our bodies as much as through our nervous system and brain.

The senses not only mediate information for the judgement of the intellect; they are also a means of igniting the imagination and of articulating sensory thought. Each form of art elaborates metaphysical and existential thought through its characteristic medium and sensory engagement. 'Any theory of painting is a metaphysics', in Merleau-Ponty's view,[100] but this statement might also be extended to the actual making of art, for every painting is itself based on implicit assumptions about the essence of the world. 'The painter "takes his body with him," says [Paul] Valéry. Indeed we cannot imagine how a mind could paint', Merleau-Ponty argues.[101]

It is similarly inconceivable that we could think of purely cerebral architecture that would not be a projection of the human body and its sensory and experiential projections and movements through space. The art of architecture is also engaged with metaphysical and existential questions concerning our being in the world. The making of architecture calls for clear thinking, but this is a specific embodied and existential mode of thought that takes place through the senses and the body, and through the specific medium of architecture. Architecture elaborates and communicates thoughts of man's incarnate confrontation with the world through 'plastic emotions', to use an expression of Le Corbusier.[102] In my view, the task of architecture is 'to make visible how the world touches us', as Merleau-Ponty said of the paintings of Paul Cézanne.[103]

The Significance of the Shadow

The eye is the organ of distance and separation, whereas touch is the sense of nearness, intimacy and affection. The eye surveys, controls and investigates, whereas touch approaches and caresses. During overpowering emotional experiences, we tend to close off the distancing sense of vision; we close the eyes when dreaming, listening to music, or caressing our beloved ones. The eye receives gestures of affections, but the hand returns them. Deep shadows and darkness are essential, because they dim the sharpness of vision, make depth and distance ambiguous and invite unconscious peripheral vision and tactile fantasy.

How much more mysterious and inviting is the street of an old town with its alternating realms of darkness and light than are the brightly and evenly lit streets of today! The imagination and daydreaming are stimulated by dim light and shadow. In order to think clearly, the sharpness of vision has to be suppressed, for thoughts travel with an absent-minded and unfocused gaze. Homogeneous bright light paralyses the imagination in the same way that homogenisation of space weakens the experience of being, and wipes away the sense of place. The human eye is most perfectly tuned for twilight rather than bright daylight.

Mist and twilight awaken the imagination by making visual images unclear and ambiguous; a Chinese painting of a foggy mountain landscape, or the raked sand garden of Ryoan-ji Zen Garden, give rise to an unfocused way of looking, evoking a trance-like, meditative state. The absent-minded gaze penetrates the surface of the physical image and focuses on infinity.

In his book *In Praise of Shadows*, Jun'ichirō Tanizaki points out that even Japanese cooking depends upon shadows, and that it is inseparable from darkness: 'And when *Y kan* is served in a lacquer dish, it is as if the darkness of the room were melting on your tongue'.[104] The writer reminds us that, in olden times, the blackened teeth of the geisha and her green–black lips as well as her white-painted face were all intended to emphasise the darkness and shadows of the room.

Likewise, the extraordinarily powerful sense of focus and presence in the paintings of Caravaggio and Rembrandt arises from the depth of shadow in which the protagonist is embedded like a precious object on a dark velvet background that absorbs all light. The shadow gives shape and life to the object in light. It also provides the realm from which fantasies and dreams arise. The art of chiaroscuro is a skill of the master architect too. In great architectural spaces, there is a constant, deep breathing of shadow and light; shadow inhales and illumination exhales light.

In our time, light has turned into a mere quantitative matter, and the window has lost its significance as a mediator between two worlds: between enclosed and open, interiority and exteriority, private and public, shadow and light. Having lost its ontological meaning, the window has turned into a mere absence of the wall. Luis Barragán, the true magician of intimate secrecy, mystery and shadow in contemporary architecture, writes:

> Take [. . .] the use of enormous plate windows [. . .] they deprive our buildings of intimacy, the effect of shadow and atmosphere. Architects all over the world have been mistaken in the proportions which they have assigned to large plate windows or spaces opening to the outside [. . .] We have lost our sense of intimate life, and have become forced to live public lives, essentially away from home.[105]

Likewise, most contemporary public spaces would become more enjoyable through a lower light intensity and its uneven distribution. The dark womb of the council chamber of Alvar Aalto's Säynätsalo Town Hall re-creates a mystical and mythological sense of community; darkness creates a sense of solidarity and strengthens the power of the spoken word. It also protects the individuality and intimacy of the Council members.

In emotional states, sense stimuli seem to shift from the more refined senses towards the more archaic, from vision down to hearing, touch and smell, and from light to shadow. A culture that seeks to control its citizens is likely to promote the opposite direction of interaction, away from intimate individuality

---

ARCHITECTURES OF HEARING AND SMELL

13 In historical towns and spaces, acoustic experiences reinforce and enrich visual experiences.

The early Cistercian Abbey of Le Thoronet in southern France, first established at Florielle in 1136, transferred to its present site in 1176. Photo: David Heald

14 In rich and invigorating experiences of places, all sensory realms interact and fuse into the memorable image of the place.

A space of smell: the spice market in Harrar, Ethiopia. Photo: Juhani Pallasmaa

13

14

and identification and towards a public and distant detachment and exposure. A society of surveillance is necessarily a society of the voyeuristic and sadistic eye. An efficient method of mental torture is the use of a constantly high level of illumination that leaves no space for mental withdrawal or privacy; even the dark interiority of self is exposed and violated.

Acoustic Intimacy

Sight isolates, whereas sound incorporates; vision is directional, whereas sound is omni-directional. The sense of sight implies exteriority, but sound creates an experience of interiority. I regard an object, but sound approaches me; the eye reaches, but the ear receives. Buildings do not react to our gaze, but they do return our sounds back to our ears. 'The centring action of sound affects man's sense of cosmos', writes Walter Ong. 'For oral cultures, the cosmos is an ongoing event with man at its centre. Man is the *umbilicus mundi*, the navel of the world'.[106] It is thought-provoking that the mental loss of the sense of centre in the contemporary world could be attributed, at least in part, to the disappearance of the integrity of the audible world.

Hearing structures and articulates the experience and understanding of space. We are not normally aware of the significance of hearing in spatial experience, although sound often provides the temporal continuum in which visual impressions are embedded. When the soundtrack is removed from a film, for instance, the scene loses its plasticity, sense of continuity and life. Silent film, indeed, had to compensate for the lack of sound by a demonstrative manner of overacting.

Adrian Stokes, the English painter and essayist, makes perceptive observations about the interaction of space and sound, sound and stone. 'Like mothers of men, the buildings are good listeners. Long sounds, distinct or seemingly in bundles, appease the orifices of palaces that lean back gradually from canal or pavement. A long sound with its echo brings consummation to the stone', he writes.[107]

Anyone who has half-woken up to the sound of a train or an ambulance in a nocturnal city, and through his/her sleep experienced the space of the city with its countless inhabitants scattered within its structures, knows the power of sound over the imagination; the nocturnal sound is a reminder of human solitude and mortality, and it makes one conscious of the entire slumbering city. Anyone who has become entranced by the sound of dripping water in the darkness of a ruin can attest to the extraordinary capacity of the ear to carve a volume into the void of darkness. The space traced by the ear in the darkness becomes a cavity sculpted directly in the interior of the mind.

The last chapter of Steen Eiler Rasmussen's seminal book *Experiencing Architecture* is significantly entitled 'Hearing Architecture'.[108] The writer describes various dimensions of acoustical qualities and recalls the acoustic percept of the underground tunnels in Vienna in Orson Welles's film *The Third Man*: 'Your ear receives the impact of both the length and the cylindrical form of the tunnel'.[109]

One can also recall the acoustic harshness of an uninhabited and unfurnished house as compared with the affability of a lived-in home, in which sound is refracted and softened by the numerous surfaces of objects of personal life. Every building or space has its characteristic sound of intimacy or monumentality, invitation or rejection, hospitality or hostility. A space is understood and appreciated through its echo as much as through its visual shape, but the acoustic percept usually remains as an unconscious background experience.

Sight is the sense of the solitary observer, whereas hearing creates a sense of connection and solidarity; our look wanders lonesomely in the dark depths of a cathedral, but the sound of the organ makes us immediately experience our affinity with the space. We stare alone at the suspense of a circus, but the burst of applause after the relaxation of suspense unites us with the crowd. The sound of church bells echoing through the streets of a town makes us aware of our citizenship. The echo of steps on a paved street has an emotional charge because the sound reverberating from surrounding walls puts us in direct interaction with space; the sound measures space and makes its scale comprehensible. We stroke the boundaries of the place and space with our ears. The cries of seagulls in the harbour awaken an awareness of the vastness of the ocean and the infiniteness of the horizon.

Every city has its echo which depends on the pattern and scale of its streets and the prevailing architectural styles and materials. The echo of a Renaissance city differs from that of a Baroque city. But our cities have lost their echo altogether. The wide, open spaces of contemporary streets do not return sound, and in the interiors of today's buildings echoes are absorbed and censored. The programmed recorded music of shopping malls and public spaces eliminates the possibility of grasping the acoustic volume of space. Our ears have been blinded.

Silence, Time and Solitude

The most essential auditory experience created by architecture is tranquillity. Architecture presents the drama of construction silenced into matter, space and light. Ultimately, architecture is the art of petrified silence. When the clutter of construction work ceases, and the shouting of workers dies away, a building becomes a museum of a waiting, patient silence. In Egyptian temples we encounter the silence that surrounded the pharaohs, in the silence of the Gothic cathedral we are reminded of the last dying note of a Gregorian chant, and the echo of Roman footsteps has just faded away from the walls of the Pantheon. Old houses take us back to the slow time and silence of the past. The silence of architecture is a responsive, remembering silence. A powerful architectural experience silences all external noise; it focuses our attention on our very existence, and as with all art, it makes us aware of our fundamental solitude.

The incredible acceleration of speed during the last century has collapsed time into the flat screen of the present, upon which the simultaneity of the world is projected. As time loses its duration, and its echo in the primordial past, man loses his sense of self as a historical being, and is threatened by the 'terror of time'.[110] Architecture emancipates us from the embrace of the present and allows us to experience the slow, healing flow of time. Buildings and cities are instruments and museums of time. They enable us to see and understand the passing of history and to participate in time cycles that surpass individual life.

Architecture connects us with the dead; through buildings we are able to imagine the bustle of the medieval street and picture a solemn procession approaching the cathedral. The time of architecture is a detained time; in the greatest of buildings time stands firmly still. In the Great Peristyle at Karnak, time has petrified into an immobile and timeless present. Time and space are eternally locked into each other in the silent spaces between these immense columns; matter, space and time fuse into one singular elemental experience, the sense of being.

The great works of modernity have forever preserved the utopian time of optimism and hope; even after decades of trying fate, they radiate an air of spring and promise. Alvar Aalto's Paimio Sanatorium is heartbreaking in its radiant belief in a humane future and the success of the societal mission of architecture. Le Corbusier's Villa Savoye makes us believe in the union of reason and beauty, ethics and aesthetics. Through periods of dramatic and tragic social and cultural change, Konstantin Melnikov's Melnikov House in Moscow has stood as a silent witness of the will and utopian spirit that once created it.

SPACES OF INTIMATE WARMTH

15 Heightened experiences of intimacy, home and protection are sensations of the naked skin.

Pierre Bonnard, *The Nude in the Bath* (detail), 1937, Musée du Petit-Palais, Paris.

16 The fireplace as an intimate and personal space of warmth.

Antoni Gaudí, Casa Batlló, Barcelona, 1904–6.

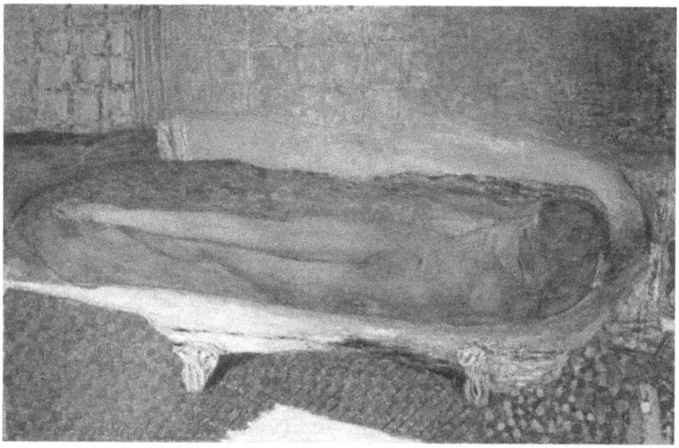
15

16

Experiencing a work of art is a private dialogue between the work and the viewer, one that excludes other interactions. 'Art is memory's *mise-en-scène*', and 'Art is made by the alone for the alone', as Cyril Connolly writes in *The Unquiet Grave*.[111] Significantly, these are sentences underlined by Luis Barragán in his copy of this book of poetry.[112] A sense of melancholy lies beneath all moving experiences of art; this is the sorrow of beauty's immaterial temporality. Art projects an unattainable ideal, the ideal of beauty that momentarily touches the eternal.

Spaces of Scent

We need only eight molecules of substance to trigger an impulse of smell in a nerve ending, and we can detect more than 10,000 different odours. The most persistent memory of any space is often its smell. I cannot remember the appearance of the door to my grandfather's farmhouse in my early childhood, but I do remember the resistance of its weight and the patina of its wood surface scarred by decades of use, and I recall especially vividly the scent of home in my farmer grandfather's house, that hit my face as an invisible wall behind the door. It was a mixture of the smells of domestic animals, the sweat of farm and domestic work, food and meals, and the wood of the all-wood house with all its furniture and objects made of wood. Every dwelling has its individual smell of home. Yet, we do not usually sense the smell of our homes, as our cells of smell have become used to it. Only when returning home after a longer absence, we again sense this specific smell of our home.

A particular smell makes us unknowingly re-enter a space completely forgotten by the retinal memory; the nostrils awaken a forgotten image, and we are enticed to enter a vivid daydream. The nose makes the eyes remember. 'Memory and imagination remain associated', as Bachelard writes; 'I alone in my memories of another century, can open the deep cupboard that still retains for me alone that unique odour, the odour of raisins, drying on a wicker tray. The odour of raisins! It is an odour that is beyond description, one that it takes a lot of imagination to smell'.[113]

What a delight to move from one realm of odour to the next, through the narrow streets of an old town! The scent sphere of a candy store makes one think of the innocence and curiosity of childhood; the dense smell of a shoemaker's workshop makes one imagine horses, saddles and harness straps and the excitement of riding; the fragrance of a bread shop projects images of health, sustenance and physical strength, whereas the perfume of a pastry shop makes one think of bourgeois felicity. Fishing towns are especially memorable because of the fusion of the smells of the sea and of the land; the powerful smell of seaweed makes one sense the depth and weight of the sea, and it turns any prosaic harbour town into the image of the lost Atlantis.

A special joy of travel is to acquaint oneself with the geography and microcosm of smells and tastes. Every city has its spectrum of tastes and odours. Sales counters on the streets are appetising exhibitions of smells: creatures of the ocean that smell of seaweed, vegetables carrying the odour of fertile earth and fruits that exude the sweet fragrance of sun and moist summer air. The menus displayed outside restaurants make us fantasise the complete course of a dinner; letters read by the eyes turn into oral sensations.

Why do abandoned houses always have the same hollow smell: is it because the particular smell is stimulated by emptiness observed by the eye? Helen Keller was able to recognise 'an old-fashioned country house because it has several levels of odors, left by a succession of families, of plants, of perfumes and draperies'.[114]

In *The Notebooks of Malte Laurids Brigge*, Rainer Maria Rilke gives a dramatic description of images of past life in an already demolished house, conveyed by traces imprinted on the wall of its neighbouring house:

> There stood the middays and the sicknesses and the exhaled breath and the smoke of years, and the sweat that breaks out under armpits and makes clothes heavy, and the stale breath of mouths, and the fusel odour of sweltering feet. There stood the tang of urine and the burn of soot and the grey reek of potatoes, and the heavy, smooth stench of ageing grease. The sweet, lingering smell of neglected infants was there, and the fearsmell of children who go to school, and the sultriness out of the beds of nubile youths.[115]

The retinal images of contemporary architecture certainly appear sterile and lifeless when compared with the emotional and associative power of the poet's olfactory imagery. The poet releases the scent and taste concealed in words. Through his words a great writer is capable of constructing an entire city with all the colours of life. But significant works of architecture also project full images of life. In fact, a great architect releases images of ideal life concealed in spaces and shapes. Le Corbusier's sketch of the suspended garden for a block of flats, with the wife beating a rug on the upper balcony, and the husband hitting a boxing bag below, as well as the fish and the electric fan on the kitchen table of the Villa Stein–de Monzie, are examples of a rare sense of life in modern images of architecture. Photographs of the Melnikov House, on the other hand, reveal a dramatic distance between the metaphysical geometry of the iconic house and the traditionally prosaic realities of life.

The Shape of Touch
'[H]ands are a complicated organism, a delta in which life from the most distant sources flows together surging into the great current of action. Hands have histories; they even have their own culture and their own particular beauty. We grant them the right to have their own development, their own wishes, feelings, moods and occupations', writes Rainer Maria Rilke in his essay on Auguste Rodin.[116] The hands are the sculptor's eyes; but they are also organs for thought, as Heidegger suggests: '[the] hand's essence can never be determined, or explained, by its being an organ which can grasp [. . .] Every motion of the hand in every one of its works carries itself through the element of thinking, every bearing of the hand bears itself in that element [. . .]'.[117]

The skin reads the texture, weight, density and temperature of matter. The surface of an old object, polished to perfection by the tool of the craftsman and the assiduous hands of its users, seduces the stroking of the hand. It is pleasurable to press a door handle shining from the thousands of hands that have entered the door before us; the clean shimmer of ageless wear has turned into an image of welcome and hospitality. The door handle is the handshake of the building. The tactile sense connects us with time and tradition: through impressions of touch we shake the hands of countless generations. A pebble polished by waves is pleasurable to the hand, not only because of its soothing shape, but because it expresses the slow process of its formation; a perfect pebble on the palm materialises duration, it is time turned into shape.

THE SIGNIFICANCE OF SHADOW AND DARKNESS

17 The face is embedded in darkness as a precious object on a dark surface of velvet.

Rembrandt, *Self-Portrait* (detail), 1660, Musée du Louvre, Paris.

18 The darkness and shadows of the Finnish peasant's house create a sense of intimacy and silence; light turns into a precious gift.

The Pertinotsa house from the late 19th century in the Seurasaari Open-Air Museum, Helsinki.
Photo: István Rácz

17 

18 

When entering the magnificent outdoor space of Louis Kahn's Salk Institute in La Jolla, California, I felt an irresistible temptation to walk directly to the concrete wall and touch the velvety smoothness and temperature of its skin. I have later learned the architect's specification for the surface and colour of the concrete: 'The matt gray of the wings of the moth'. Our skin traces temperature spaces with unerring precision; the cool and invigorating shadow under a tree, or the caressing sphere of warmth in a spot of sun, turn into experiences of space and place. In my childhood images of the Finnish countryside, I can vividly recall walls against the angle of the sun, walls which multiplied the heat of radiation and melted the snow, allowing the first smell of pregnant soil to announce the approach of summer. These early pockets of spring were identified by the skin and the nose as much as by the eye.

Gravity is measured by the bottom of the foot; we trace the density and texture of the ground through our soles. Standing barefoot on a smooth glacial rock by the sea at sunset and sensing the warmth of the sun-heated stone through one's soles is an extraordinarily healing experience, making one part of the eternal cycle of nature. One senses the slow breathing of the earth.

'In our houses we have nooks and corners in which we like to curl up comfortably. To curl up belongs to the phenomenology of the verb to inhabit, and only those who have learned to do so can inhabit with intensity', writes Bachelard.[118] 'And always, in our daydreams, the house is a large cradle', he continues.[119]

There is a strong identity between naked skin and the sensation of home. The experience of home is essentially an experience of intimate warmth. The space of warmth around a fireplace is the space of ultimate intimacy and comfort. Marcel Proust gives a poetic description of such a fireside space, as sensed by the skin: 'It is like an immaterial alcove, a warm cave carved into the room itself, a zone of hot weather with floating boundaries'.[120] Antonio Gaudi's fireplace in Casa Battló in Barcelona is an alcove of warmth, which one enters and occupies.

A sense of homecoming has never been stronger for me than when seeing a light in the window of my childhood house in a snow-covered landscape at dusk, the memory of the warm interior already gently warming my frozen limbs. 'A light in the window is a waiting light', Bachelard writes.[121] Home and the pleasure of the skin turn into a singular sensation.

The Taste of Stone

In his writings, Adrian Stokes was particularly sensitive to the realms of tactile and oral sensations: 'In employing smooth and rough as generic terms of architectural dichotomy I am better able to preserve both the oral and the tactile notions that underlie the visual. There is a hunger of the eyes, and doubtless there has been some permeation of the visual sense, as of touch, by the once all-embracing oral impulse'.[122] Stokes writes also about the 'oral invitation of Veronese marble',[123] and he quotes a letter of John Ruskin: 'I should like to eat up this Verona touch by touch'.[124]

There is a subtle transference between tactile and taste experiences. Vision becomes transferred to taste as well; certain colours and delicate details evoke oral sensations. A delicately coloured polished stone surface is subliminally sensed by the tongue. Our sensory experience of the world originates in the interior sensation of the mouth, and the world tends to return to its oral origins. The most archaic origin of architectural space is in the cavity of the mouth, through which the infant first experiences the world.

Many years ago, when visiting the DL James House in Carmel, California, designed by Charles and Henry Greene, I felt compelled to kneel and touch the delicately shining white marble threshold of the front door with my tongue. The sensuous materials and skilfully crafted details of Carlo Scarpa's architecture as well as the sensuous colours of Luis Barragán's houses frequently evoke oral experiences. Deliciously coloured surfaces of *stucco lustro*, a highly polished colour or wood surfaces also present themselves to the appreciation of the tongue.

Jun'ichirō Tanizaki describes impressively the spatial qualities of the sense of taste, and the subtle interaction of the senses in the simple act of uncovering a bowl of soup:

> With lacquerware there is a beauty in that moment between removing the lid and lifting the bowl to the mouth when one gazes at the still, silent liquid in the dark depths of the bowl, its colour hardly differing from the bowl itself. What lies within the darkness one cannot distinguish, but the palm senses the gentle movements of the liquid, vapor rises from within forming droplets on the rim, and a fragrance carried upon the vapour brings a delicate anticipation. [. . .] A moment of mystery, it might almost be called, a moment of trance.[125]

A fine architectural space opens up and presents itself with the same fullness of experience as Tanizaki's bowl of soup. Architectural experience brings the world into a most intimate contact with the body.

Images of Muscle and Bone

As a bird building its nests, primitive man used his own body as the dimensioning and proportioning system of his constructions. The essential skills of making a living in traditional cultures are based on the wisdom of the body stored in the haptic memory. The essential knowledge and skill of the ancient hunter, fisherman and farmer, as well as of the mason and stone cutter, was an imitation of an embodied tradition of the trade, stored in the muscular and tactile senses. Skill was learned through incorporating the sequence of movements refined by tradition, not through words or theory.

The body knows and remembers. Architectural meaning derives from archaic responses and reactions remembered by the body and the senses. Architecture has to respond to traits of primordial behaviour preserved and passed down by the genes. It does not only respond to the functional and conscious intellectual and social needs of today's city dweller; it must also remember the primordial hunter and farmer concealed in the human body. Our sensations of comfort, protection and home are rooted in the primordial experiences of countless generations. Bachelard calls these 'images that bring out the primitiveness in us', or 'primal images'.[126] He writes of the strength of the bodily memory:

> [T]he house we were born in has engraved within us the hierarchy of the various functions of inhabiting. We are the diagram of the functions of inhabiting that particular house, and all the other houses are but variations on a fundamental theme. The word habit is too worn a word to express this passionate liaison of our bodies, which do not forget, with an unforgettable house.[127]

Modern architecture has had its own conscience in recognising a bias towards the visual nature of designs. 'Architecture of the exterior seems to have interested architects of the avant-garde at the expense of architecture of the interior. As if a house were to be conceived for the pleasure of the eye rather than for the wellbeing of the inhabitants', writes Eileen Gray,[128] whose design approach seems to grow from a study of the minute situations of daily life rather than visual and compositional preconceptions.

VISION AND HAPTICITY

19 A tactile ingredient is concealed in vision.

Bronze figure from Mongolia, 15th century, State Public Library, Ulan Bator, Mongolia. The Buddhist goddess Tara possesses five additional eyes, on the forehead and in her hands and feet. These are considered as signs of enlightenment.

20 The door pull is the handshake of a building, which can be inviting and courteous, or forbidding and aggressive.

Alvar Aalto, The Iron House, Helsinki, 1954: door pulls. Photo: Heikki Havas

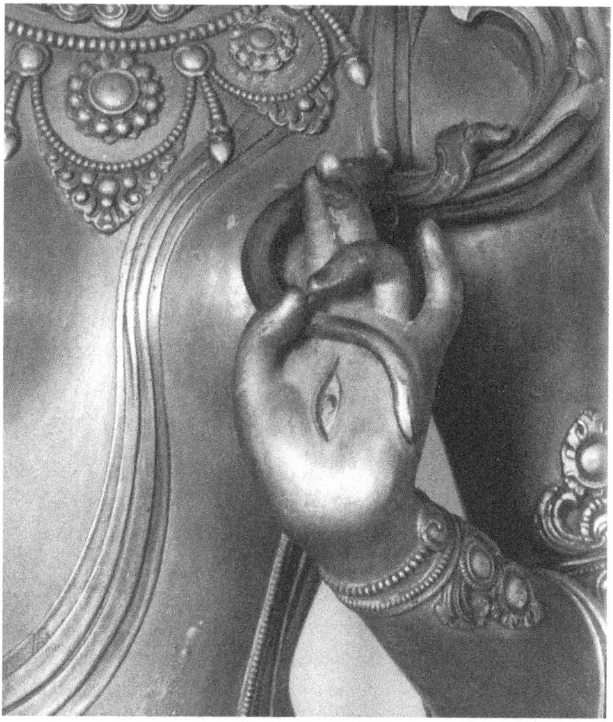
19

20

Architecture cannot, however, become an instrument of mere functionality, bodily comfort and sensory pleasure without losing its existentially mediating task. A distinct sense of distance, resistance and tension has to be maintained in relation to programme, function and comfort. A piece of architecture should not become transparent in its utilitarian and rational motives; it has to maintain its impenetrable secret and mystery in order to ignite our imagination and emotions.

Tadao Ando has expressed a desire for a tension or opposition between functionality and uselessness in his work: 'I believe in removing architecture from function after ensuring the observation of functional basis. In other words, I like to see how far architecture can pursue function and then, after the pursuit has been made, to see how far architecture can be removed from function. The significance of architecture is found in the distance between it and function'.[129]

Images of Action

Stepping stones set in the grass of a garden are images and imprints of footsteps. As we open a door, the body weight meets the weight of the door; the legs measure the steps as we ascend a stairway, the hand strokes the handrail and the entire body moves diagonally and dramatically through space.

There is an inherent suggestion of action in images of architecture, the moment of active encounter, or a 'promise of function'[130] and purpose. 'The objects which surround my body reflect its possible action upon them', writes Henri Bergson.[131] It is this possibility of action that separates architecture from other forms of art. As a consequence of this implied action, a bodily reaction is an inseparable aspect of the experience of architecture. A meaningful architectural experience is not simply a series of retinal images. The 'elements' of architecture are not visual units or Gestalt; they are encounters, confrontations that interact with expectations and memory. 'In such memory, the past is embodied in actions. Rather than being contained separately somewhere in the mind or brain, it is actively an ingredient in the very bodily movements that accomplish a particular action', Edward Casey writes of the interplay of memory and actions.[132]

The experience of home is structured by distinct activities – cooking, eating, socialising, reading, storing, sleeping and intimate acts – not by visual elements. A building is encountered; it is approached, confronted, related to one's body, moved around and through and utilised as a condition for other things. Architecture initiates, directs and organises behaviour and movement. A building is not an end in itself; it frames, articulates, structures, gives significance, relates, separates and unites, facilitates and prohibits. Consequently, basic architectural experiences have a verb form rather than being nouns. Authentic architectural experiences consist then, for instance, of approaching or confronting a building, rather than the formal apprehension of a facade; of the act of entering, and not simply the visual design of the door; of looking in or out through a window, rather than the window itself as a material object; or of occupying the sphere of warmth, rather than the fireplace as an object of visual design. Architectural space is lived space rather than physical space, and lived space always transcends geometry and measurability.

In his analysis of Fra Angelico's *Annunciation* in the charming essay 'From the Doorstep to the Common Room' (1926), Alvar Aalto recognises the *verb-essence* of architectural experience by speaking of the act of *entering* the room, not of the formal design of the porch or the door.[133]

Modern architectural theory and critique have had a strong tendency to regard space as an immaterial object delineated by material surfaces, instead of understanding space in terms of dynamic interactions and interrelations. In many books on architectural theory an architectural space, say the interior space of St Peter's in Rome, is presented as a positive material cast of the void of the space. A void and a material volume are experientially totally exclusive. Japanese thinking, however, is founded on a relational understanding of the concept of space. In recognition of the verb-essence of the architectural experience, Professor Fred Thompson uses the notions of 'spacing' instead of 'space', and of 'timing' instead of 'time', in his essay on the concept of *Ma*, and the unity of space and time in Japanese thinking.[134] He aptly describes units of architectural experience with gerunds, or verb-nouns.

Bodily Identification

The authenticity of architectural experience is grounded in the tectonic language of building and the comprehensibility of the act of construction to the senses. We behold, touch, listen and measure the world with our entire bodily existence, and the experiential world becomes organised and articulated around the centre of the body. Our domicile is the refuge of our body, memory and identity. We are in constant dialogue and interaction with the environment, to the degree that it is impossible to detach the image of the self from its spatial and situational existence. 'I am my body', Gabriel Marcel claims,[135] but 'I am the space, where I am', establishes the poet Noël Arnaud.[136]

Henry Moore writes perceptively of the necessity of bodily identification in the making of sculpture:

> This is what the sculptor must do. He must strive continually to think of, and use, form in its full spatial completeness. He gets the solid shape, as it were, inside his head – he thinks of it, whatever its size, as if he were holding it completely enclosed in the hollow of his hand. He mentally visualizes a complex form from all round itself; he knows while he looks at one side what the other side is like; he identifies himself with its centre of gravity, its mass, its weight; he realizes its volume, and the space that the shape displaces in the air.[137]

The encounter of any work of art implies a bodily interaction. The painter Graham Sutherland expresses this view on the artist's work: 'In a sense the landscape painter must almost look at the landscape as if it were himself – himself as a human being'.[138] In Cézanne's view, 'the landscape thinks itself in me, and I am its consciousness'.[139] A work of art functions as another person, with whom one unconsciously converses. When confronting a work of art, we project our emotions and feelings onto the work. A curious exchange takes place; we lend the work our emotions, whereas the work lends us its authority, aura and enigma. Eventually, we meet ourselves in the work. Melanie Klein's notion of 'projective identification' suggests that, in fact, all human interaction implies projection of fragments of the self onto the other person.[140]

Mimesis of the Body

A great musician plays himself rather than the instrument, and a skilful soccer player plays the entity of himself, the other players and the internalised and embodied field, instead of merely kicking the ball. 'The player understands where the goal is in a way which is lived rather than known. The mind does not inhabit the playing field but the field is inhabited by a "knowing" body', writes Richard Lang when commenting on Merleau-Ponty's views on the skills of playing soccer.[141]

Similarly, during the design process, the architect gradually internalises the landscape, the entire context, and the functional requirements as well as his/her conceived building: movement, balance and scale are felt unconsciously

PERIPHERAL VISION AND A SENSE OF INTERIORITY

21 The forest enfolds us in its multisensory embrace. The multiplicity of peripheral stimuli effectively pulls us into the reality of its space.

Finnish pine forest in the vicinity of Alvar Aalto's Villa Mairea, Noormarkku. Photo: Rauno Träskelin

22 The scale and painterly technique of American Expressionist painters provide peripheral stimuli and invite us into the space

Jackson Pollock, *One: Number 31, 1950* (detail), 1950, Museum of Modern Art, New York.

21

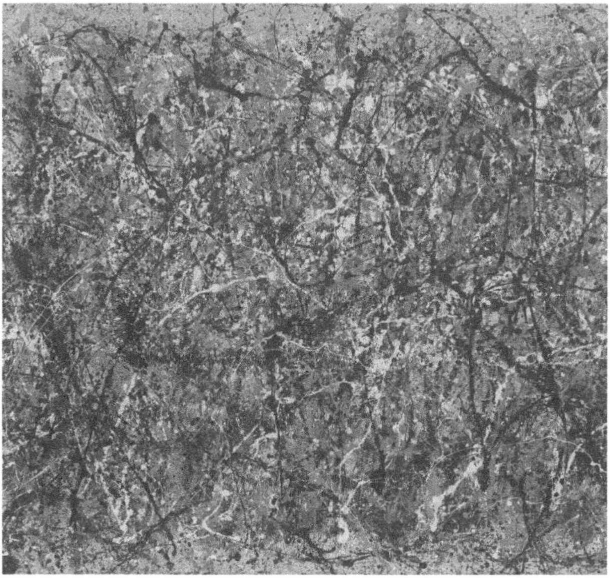
22

through the body as tensions in the muscular system and in the positions of the skeleton and inner organs. Even as a rough preliminary sketch, the projected building is imaginatively experienced as part of the existential life world, not as an isolated abstraction. As the work interacts with the body of the observer, the experience mirrors the bodily sensations of the maker. Consequently, architecture is communication from the body of the architect directly to the body of the person who encounters the work, perhaps centuries later.

Understanding architectural scale implies the unconscious measuring of the object or the building with one's body, and of projecting one's body scheme into the place and space in question. We feel pleasure and protection when the body discovers its resonance in space. When experiencing a structure, we unconsciously mimic its configuration with our bones and muscles: also, the pleasurably animated flow of a piece of music is subconsciously transformed into bodily sensations, the composition of an abstract painting is experienced as tensions in the muscular system, and the structures of a building are unconsciously imitated and comprehended through the skeletal system. Unknowingly, we perform the task of the column or of the vault with our body. 'The brick wants to become an arch', as Louis Kahn said, and this metamorphosis takes place through the mimetic capacity of the body.[142]

The sense of gravity is the essence of all architectonic structures, and great architecture makes us aware of gravity and earth; architecture may re-enforce the sense of weight or make the material float or soar. Architecture arises from horizontality, but it strengthens the experience of the vertical dimension of the

---

LIFE-ENHANCING ARCHITECTURE OF THE SENSES

23 An architecture of formal restraint with a rare sensuous richness addressing all the senses simultaneously.

Peter Zumthor, Thermal Baths, Vals, Graubünden, Switzerland, 1990–6. Photo: Hélène Binet

24 An architecture that addresses our sense of movement and touch as much as the eye, and creates an ambience of domesticity and welcome.

Alvar Aalto, Villa Mairea, Noormarkku, 1938–9: entry hall, living room and main staircase. Photo: Rauno Träskelin

23

24

world. At the same time as making us aware of the depth of the earth, it makes us dream of levitation and flight.

Spaces of Memory and Imagination

We have an innate capacity for remembering and imagining places. The philosophers of classical Greece already understood the grounding significance of place. 'Everything in the human world is placed'.[143] Perception, memory and imagination are in constant interaction; the domain of presence fuses into images of memory and fantasy. We keep constructing an immense city of evocation and remembrance, and all the cities we have visited are precincts in this metropolis of the mind.

Literature and cinema would be devoid of their power of enchantment without our capacity to *enter* a remembered or imagined place. The spaces and places enticed by a work of art are real in the full sense of the experience. 'Tintoretto did not choose that yellow rift in the sky above Golgotha to signify anguish or to provoke it. It is anguish and yellow sky at the same time. Not sky of anguish or anguished sky; it is an anguish become thing, anguish which has turned into yellow-rift of sky', writes Sartre of the painter's 'Golgotha'.[144] Similarly, the architecture of Michelangelo does not present symbols of melancholy; his buildings actually mourn. When experiencing a work of art, a curious exchange takes place; the work projects its aura, and we project our own emotions and perceptions onto the work. The melancholy in Michelangelo's architecture is fundamentally the viewer's sense of his/her own melancholy enticed by the authority of the art work. Enigmatically, we encounter ourselves in the work; we are moved by our own associations and emotions.

Memory takes us back to distant cities, and novels transport us through cities invoked by the magic of the writer's word. The rooms, squares and streets of a great writer are as vivid as any that we have visited; the invisible cities of Italo Calvino have forever enriched the urban geography of the world. The city of San Francisco unfolds in its multiplicity through the montage of Hitchcock's *Vertigo*; we *enter* the haunting edifices in the steps of the protagonist and see them through his eyes. We *become* citizens of mid-19th-century St Petersburg through the incantations of Dostoyevsky. We *are* in the room of Raskolnikov's shocking double murder, we *are* among the terrified spectators watching Mikolka and his drunken friends beat a horse to death in the street, frustrated by our inability to prevent the insane and purposeless cruelty.

The cities of filmmakers, built up of momentary fragments, envelop us with the full vigour of real cities. The streets in great paintings continue around corners and past the edges of the picture frame into the invisible with all the intricacies of life. '[The painter] makes [houses], that is, he creates an imaginary house on the canvas and not a sign of a house. And the house which thus appears preserves all the ambiguity of real houses', writes Sartre.[145]

There are cities that remain mere distant visual images when remembered, and cities that are remembered in all their vivacity. The memory re-evokes the delightful city with all its sounds and smells and variations of light and shade. I can even choose whether to walk on the sunny side or the shaded side of the street in the pleasurable city of my remembrance. The real measure of the qualities of a city is whether one can imagine falling in love in it.

An Architecture of the Senses

Various architectures can be distinguished on the basis of the sense modality they tend to emphasise. Alongside the prevailing architecture of the eye, there is a haptic architecture of the muscle and the skin. There is architecture that also recognises the realms of hearing, smell and taste.

The architectures of Le Corbusier and Richard Meier, for instance, clearly favour sight, either as a frontal encounter, or the kinaesthetic eye of the *promenade architecturale* (even if the later works of Le Corbusier incorporate strong tactile experiences in the forceful presence of materiality and weight). On the other hand, the architecture of the Expressionist orientation, beginning with Erich Mendelsohn and Hans Scharoun, favours muscular and haptic plasticity as a consequence of the suppression of ocular perspectival dominance. Frank Lloyd Wright's and Alvar Aalto's architectures are based on a full recognition of the embodied human condition and of the multitude of instinctual reactions hidden in the human unconscious. In today's architecture, the multitude of sensory experiences is heightened in the work of Glenn Murcutt, Steven Holl and Peter Zumthor, for instance.

Alvar Aalto was consciously concerned with all the senses in his architecture. His comment on the sensory intentions in his furniture design clearly reveals this concern: 'A piece of furniture that forms a part of a person's daily habitat should not cause excessive glare from light reflection: ditto, it should not be disadvantageous in terms of sound, sound absorption, etc. A piece that comes into the most intimate contact with man, as a chair does, shouldn't be constructed of materials that are excessively good conductors of heat'.[146] Aalto was clearly more interested in the encounter of the object and the body of the user than in mere visual aesthetics.

Aalto's architecture exhibits a muscular and haptic presence. It incorporates dislocations, skew confrontations, irregularities and polyrhythms in order to arouse bodily, muscular and haptic experiences. His elaborate surface textures and details, crafted for the hand, invite the sense of touch and create an atmosphere of intimacy and warmth; this architecture approaches you as an individual, as if it had been conceived for you alone. Instead of the disembodied Cartesian idealism of the architecture of the eye, Aalto's architecture is based on sensory realism. His buildings are not based on a single dominant concept or Gestalt; rather, they are sensory agglomerations. They sometimes even appear clumsy and unresolved as drawings, but they are conceived to be appreciated in their actual physical and spatial encounter, 'in the flesh' of the lived world, not as constructions of idealised vision.

The Task of Architecture

The timeless task of architecture is to create embodied and lived existential metaphors that concretise and structure our being in the world. Architecture reflects, materialises and eternalises ideas and images of ideal life. Buildings and towns enable us to structure, understand and remember the shapeless flow of reality and, ultimately, to recognise and remember who we are. Architecture enables us to perceive and understand the dialectics of permanence and change, past and present, to settle ourselves in the world, and to place ourselves in the continuum of culture and time.

In its way of representing and structuring action and power, societal and cultural order, interaction and separation, identity and memory, architecture is engaged with fundamental existential questions. All experience implies the acts of recollecting, remembering and comparing. An embodied memory has an essential role as the basis of remembering a space or a place. We transfer all the cities and towns that we have visited, all the places that we have recognised, into the incarnate memory of our body. Our domicile becomes integrated with our self-identity; it becomes part of our own body and being.

In memorable experiences of architecture, place, matter and time fuse into one singular dimension, into the basic substance of being, the existential experience, that penetrates our consciousness. We identify ourselves with this space, this place and this moment, and these dimensions become ingredients of our very existence. Architecture is the art of reconciliation between ourselves and the world, and this mediation takes place through the senses.

In 1954, at the age of 85, Frank Lloyd Wright formulated the mental task of architecture in the following words:

> What is needed most in architecture today is the very thing that is most needed in life – Integrity. Just as it is in a human being, so integrity is the deepest quality in a building [. . .] If we succeed, we will have done a great service to our moral nature – the psyche – of our democratic society [. . .] Stand up for integrity in your building and you stand for integrity not only in the life of those who did the building, but socially a reciprocal relationship is inevitable.[147]

This emphatic declaration of architecture's mission is even more urgent today than at the time of its writing seven decades ago. And this view calls for a full understanding of the human condition.

A DOOR HANDLE, A HANDSHAKE

AN INTRODUCTION TO JUHANI PALLASMAA AND HIS WORK

PETER MACKEITH

In much the same way that a door handle is the 'handshake' of a building, this book provides an opportunity to shake the hand of the Finnish architect, educator and author Juhani Pallasmaa – even to share a few moments in his company. *The Eyes of the Skin* is very much a book for the hand; like its author, the book's narrative has an intimate grasp, gently encouraging your curiosity. The qualities of warmth, intelligence, generosity, courtesy and inspiration in the author's voice emerge rapidly and reward your engagement.

As a designer, Pallasmaa has given great attention to the design and fabrication of door handles. Similar to his predecessors in the Nordic architectural culture, among them Eliel Saarinen (1873–1950), Erik Gunnar Asplund (1885–1940), Arne Jacobsen (1902–1971) and Alvar Aalto (1898–1976), the door handle possesses talismanic significance for the architect and is a primary detail to be explored, refined and crafted. Pages of Pallasmaa's sketchbooks depict multiple, obsessive design iterations of a lever handle, for instance, and a cast bronze, gently-curved vertical door pull installed in his home city of Helsinki contains all the elements, formal principles and ambitions of an entire building commission. The anthropomorphic analogy to *The Eyes of the Skin* is intensely appropriate: in the book's clear structure, intellectual density, precise articulation, humane sensitivity and profound meaning, there can be discerned the character of the author.

The equivalence between a designed door handle and a published book is emblematic, for Pallasmaa's life and work more generally highlights the complementary relationship between "thinking" and "making", between the act of writing on architecture and the act of designing and constructing architecture. Although Pallasmaa describes his trajectory into education and his work as an essayist and critic as a "slow, unintentional drift", parallel to his work as an architect, he is quite resolute about his critical perspective and his writing process – as a practising architect, exploring ideas:

> 'I write about art, architecture and the life world as a practicing architect and designer who is also engaged in the realm of the arts. I write in the same manner and with the same intentions as I sketch and draw, open mindedly and without preconceptions or pre-set ideas. The words arise in the same manner as the lines of a drawing unfold, semi-automatically, revealing an image that has been hiding somewhere in the folds of thoughts, associations and embodied memories. Both the drawing and the sentence seek to give a shape to an emergent feeling, a shapeless complex of uncertainty and intuitive assurance that acquires intentionality and meaning at the moment of its very emergence. As a consequence of my way of working, a design and an essay are the same thing for me, yet they seem to be causally unrelated and exist in different realities, as two parallel but independent products or observations of the mind'.[1]

1. Juhani Pallasmaa at the age of four on his farmer grandfather's horse-drawn mower, manufactured in the mid-1930s. Photographer unknown.

2. Juhani Pallasmaa at the age of seventy five. Photo: Knut Thyberg.

The Eyes of the Skin thus has this tangible architectural intentionality behind it. First published in 1996, the book was produced in a second edition in 2005, a third edition in 2012, and is now being re-issued again in this fourth edition, in both print and digital versions. Indeed, you may in fact hold in your hands a digital reader, having only seconds ago downloaded the digital file to your LED screen. Ironically, at one point after *The Eyes of the Skin*'s first printing had sold through, the book circulated in seemingly endless photocopied versions, each a paler reflection of its *samizdat* predecessor. But no matter, neither form of contemporary technological reproduction can obscure the fact that this is still a book, written, designed and scaled for your hands as much as for your eyes. Indeed, this is a book originally, laboriously and intentionally written by hand, through many manuscript drafts and revisions, as Pallasmaa describes: 'I . . . write in the same way as I design, through eight to ten successive long-hand manuscripts, or hand-made corrections, that my secretary types and hands back to me for further additions and corrections. I need to see my own, almost illegible handwriting on the paper in order to feel an intimacy and internalization with the text. I also appreciate the signs and traces of work'.[2]

Read the book's relatively few pages then with this manual sensibility, as a material, tangible, even sensual, condensation of thought and feeling – and time. For no matter the swiftness of your acquisition of the book, and despite the book's brevity (you might finish its xx pages in an hour), like all works of literary ambition, *The Eyes of the Skin* absolutely intends to hold your attention and slow your sense of time and experience as you turn the pages. You may find yourself, as many have, subsequently returning to it again and again, extending the book's actual duration well past the moment you first turned the last page.

This depth and duration is layered intellectually, historically and culturally. In shaking Pallasmaa's hand, in *The Eyes of the Skin*, you also encounter his friends and mentors – and this, it must be said, is a long line of diverse companions. Be prepared for some depth and disorientation here, too: he's fond of quoting Aldo van Eyck's assertion that his own conversation with both Cezanne and Giotto was ongoing, even if the painters had passed away hundreds of years ago! In Pallasmaa's view, 'One's most important teacher may have died half a millennium ago; one's true mentor could well be Filippo Brunelleschi or Piero della Francesca. I believe that every serious artist – at the edge of his/her consciousness – addresses and offers his/her work to a superior colleague for approval. If you feel that your work is approved by Filippo or Piero, or, for instance, it cannot be entirely worthless'.[3]

Unquestionably, in this vein, *The Eyes of the Skin* has both its antecedents and companions in Nordic architectural thinking; these are well worth considering. Asplund and Aalto's fascination with the tactile and telling detail has been mentioned, but for Pallasmaa, Aalto's depiction of Asplund (in a 1940 memorial for the Swedish architect) as the modern architect who uncovered and insisted on architecture's 'psychological' character is just as important. Pallasmaa also identifies Aalto's prescient observation on the need for modern architecture to address human, psychological qualities: '. . .the fault is that the rationalization has not gone deep enough. Instead of resisting the rationalist approach, the latest phase of modern architecture is trying to channel rational methods away from the technical sphere and into that of humanism and

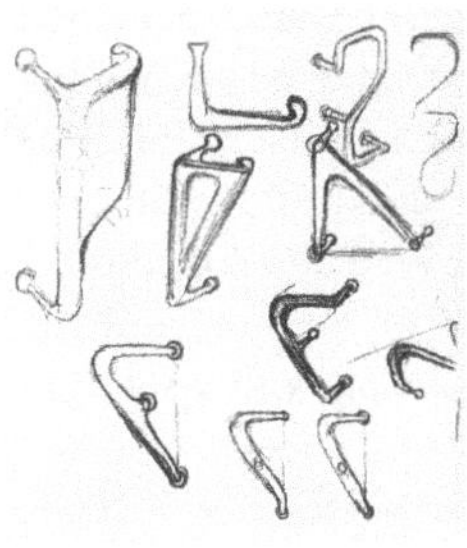

3. Sketches for door pulls, early 1990s. Page in a sketch book.

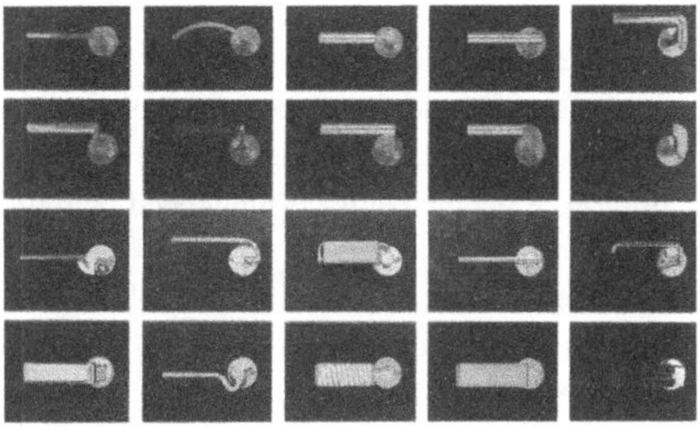

4. Prototypes for door handles, 1991. The set of twenty variations was produced for Pallasmaa's exhibition in the Finland Pavilion at the Venice Biennale in 1991. Source: From Rauno Träskelin.

psychology'.[4] The Danish professor Steen Eiler Rasmussen's elegant *Experiencing Architecture*, published in 1959, is a progenitor in the assertion of architecture's sensory qualities.[5] The presence of Pallasmaa's direct Finnish mentors, Aulis Blomstedt and Aarno Ruusuvuori, can be sensed in the book's demanding insistence on a probity for architecture. Sigurd Lewerentz (1885–1975), Asplund's former collaborator, also has an intriguing role in the book's DNA, by virtue of his late works of the 1960s, the singular, evocative brick-constructed churches of St Peter and St Mark in Klippan and Bjorkhagen, Sweden.[6] The Norwegian academic Christian Norberg-Schulz emphasized existential and phenomenological issues – "an ontology of place", drawing heavily upon Martin Heidegger's philosophical reflections – in examining architecture's history and possibilities through a series of books and essays written primarily in the 1970s and 1980s; Pallasmaa's thinking in *The Eyes of the Skin* animates and specifies Norberg-Schulz's studies.[7] And as importantly in the Nordic fraternity, Sverre Fehn's poetic works (1924–2009), thoughts and character – so brilliantly condensed by Per Olaf Fjeld in *The Thought of Construction* (1984) – parallel Pallasmaa's own emergence in the same decade.[8]

But to position the book solely in a Nordic architectural and intellectual lineage is to sequester it unfairly as a 'regionalist' outlook, simply an expression borne of Ultima Thule. Pallasmaa is too well-read, well-travelled and well-acquainted to be so simply defined. The book is also an implicit introduction to two significant British architects and educators, Colin St John Wilson (1922–2007) and Kenneth Frampton (b 1930), both close friends of Pallasmaa, each with their affinities for Finnish and Nordic architecture and each with their own post-war trajectory of humanist intellectual production (and, in Wilson's case, with significant architectural accomplishments). Wilson, the deeply read former Dean of Architecture at Cambridge, maintained a lifelong stubborn, sensitive insistence on a philosophical, ethical ground for architecture; in parallel, he identified and upheld "the other tradition" of modern architecture – championing Aalto, Scharoun, Eileen Gray, Asplund and Lewerentz as architects of the 20th century who were never bound by dogmatic definitions of function or form.[9] As importantly, Wilson introduced Pallasmaa to the psychologically grounded writings of the art critic Adrian Stokes.[10] Frampton, as deeply read and influenced by the Frankfurt School of post-war political, economic and social thought, became one of the canonical late 20th-century historians of modern architecture; beginning with a series of seminal essays in the early 1980s, he set out an agenda for an architecture of 'critical regionalism', in which the work of Aalto, Jorn Utzon (1918–2008), Fehn and others across the globe demonstrated site- and culture-specificity.[11] For Pallasmaa, already engaged in conversations with Wilson and Frampton by the late 1970s and throughout the 1980s, these perspectives proved deeply affective and influential.

Intertwined amongst this intellectual development and sourcing is an equally strong set of North American voices. The long-time Dean of the Cooper Union School of Architecture, John Hejduk (1929–2000), had befriended Pallasmaa already in the late 1970s – along with supporting Sverre Fehn – and their shared understanding was of a poetic imperative for architecture. To similar effect, a young Daniel Libeskind had welcomed Pallasmaa to the Architecture Studio at the Cranbrook Academy during his leadership tenure there; the two began a correspondence, an exchange of drawings and exhibitions, and a mutually supportive personal and professional relationship. Importantly, Pallasmaa credits Libeskind with introducing him to Gaston Bachelard's book *The Poetics of Space* – a transformative moment, as Pallasmaa acknowledges.[12]

As Pallasmaa's own introduction makes clear, the direct origins of *The Eyes of the Skin* lie in the mutuality of ideas, perspectives and approaches initiated and shared in the early 1990s between the American architect and educator Steven Holl, the Mexican-Canadian academic Alberto Pėrez-Gómez (first resident at Carleton University and then at McGill University in Canada) and Pallasmaa. All three were drawn together, in thought and practice, by their ambitions to ground architecture in a phenomenological approach, in a quietly dramatic counterpoint to the prevailing dictates of architecture culture at the time – the eclipse of Euclidean geometry, for instance, or the de-centring of the human subject, or the undecidability of meaning.

From their first meeting at the 1991 Alvar Aalto Symposium in Finland, Holl and Pallasmaa had immediately shared such common perspectives. The two had further bonded in succeeding years as Holl was awarded through competition the commission for Museum of Contemporary Art in Helsinki, the building now known by its competition motto *Kiasma* (the word itself a Fennicised spelling of a Merleau-Ponty concept).[13] Pallasmaa would assist Holl's commission in Finland as associate architect and would contribute to the site planning and public space design of the building. Perez-Gomez, no less, through his seminal work *Architecture and the Crisis of Modern Science* and subsequent publications, pursued similar intensely researched and deeply felt agendas; Pallasmaa was a regular contributor to and participant in Perez-Gomez' doctoral program in architectural history and theory at McGill.[14]

In this phenomenological grounding, the works of the 20th-century French *philosophes* Gaston Bachelard and Maurice Merleau-Ponty figure prominently (along with the more sheerly poetic inspirations of Rainer Maria Rilke, Joseph Brodsky and Jorge Luis Borges).[15] Pallasmaa acknowledges his clear debts to both Bachelard and Merleau-Ponty in his writings and lectures, declaring Bachelard's writings "a kind of lodestone" and Merleau-Ponty's perspectives "inspiringly open-ended and optimistic".

Despite this layered heritage, *The Eyes of the Skin* was first envisioned as a singular intellectual and deeply felt essay, but has since engendered two further, related volumes, *The Thinking Hand* and *The Embodied Image*.[16] While you might be drawn towards these essays by this first reading, the book can nonetheless be read entirely on its own. Entirely on its own, provided you are also willing to enter the fantastic library of extended references the book both names and suggests, as well as the larger world of artistic works and architectural locations it specifies and evokes. Indeed, the selected images and extensive endnotes of the book are merely a pale reflection of the immense personal library of references from which Pallasmaa draws.

That library, in fact, is a real space – for many who visit with Pallasmaa in his Helsinki office, it is the central room and the primary space for discussion, entertainment and intellectual and visual references. Pallasmaa is a bibliophile, as so many architects are, and the bookshelves lining the library have now expanded into the entry corridor and as well, into the other office studio rooms. There is always a stack of newly acquired books on the library's main table, as well as several other stacks set aside as references for ongoing essays and lecture preparation. The cataloguing of the library is a Sisyphean task; it was often the introductory task for the newest member of the office staff and entailed intense discussions as to cataloguing classification systems. For Pallasmaa, as with Thomas Jefferson (the intellectual and amateur architect), his library's shelving required a re-conceptualisation of the order of knowledge: 'Until the age of forty, I used to classify my books in two categories: architecture books and other books. Then I realized that my first category mostly dealt

5. Prototypes for drawer and door pulls, cast bronze, 1991.
Source: From Rauno Träskelin.

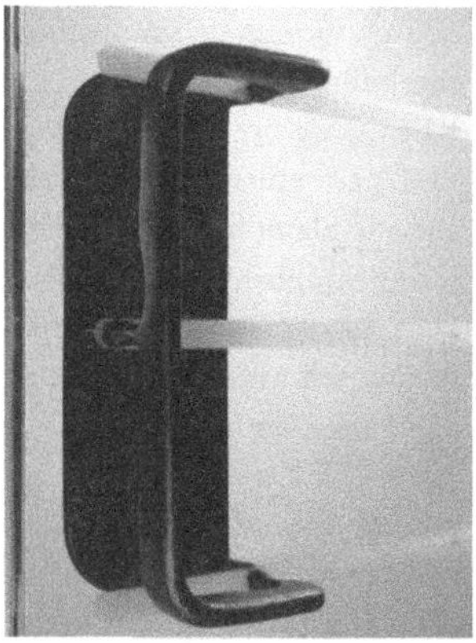

6. Door pull and push for the glass doors of Marimekko Shop in Helsinki. Patinated cast bronze, 1986.
Source: From Rauno Träskelin.

with architecture as an aestheticized formalism, whereas the second category posed cities, buildings and settings as integrated with life and human character. During the past thirty years, I have all books as architecture book, because all human situations, histories, fictions, actions, and thoughts are framed by human constructions and artifacts; our spatial, material and mental constructions provide essential horizons of understanding. I read poems, listen to music, look at paintings, and watch films as potential architectural propositions'.[17]

But this is not the reflective solitude of Saint Jerome in his library cell. The Pallasmaa library has also been the location since 1994 – roughly the time of *The Eyes of the Skin*'s conception and writing – of a conversation group drawn from across the intellectual, artistic and cultural life of Finland, including "a poet, a cultural historian, a theater director, a composer, a dramaturge, a painter, a photographer, and two literary critics. . ."[18] Here, too, the inclusiveness is telling; Pallasmaa's desire is to see the interrelationships and layers of knowledge and perspective.

Accept *The Eyes of the Skin* then as an open-handed invitation to this library and to this conversation group, as an encouraging hand beckoning and pointing towards an expanded territory of history and culture. This, too, is an ambition of the book: to situate and ground considerations of architecture responsibly (and responsively) within that larger cultural territory and simultaneously, to engage you to that larger culture as well. Importantly, this is a conversation and a reading that needs no translator: as with all his commissioned work for primarily English-speaking audiences, Pallasmaa has written *The Eyes of the Skin* in English from the beginning. His fluency is second nature, and while the essay's tone may vary from the analytical to the conditional to the declarative, the author's language is of the first order.

The book may possess another manuality altogether for you. Franz Kafka provocatively asserted that: 'a book must be an ice ax to break the seas frozen inside our soul'.[19] The author of *The Eyes of the Skin* might offer a gentler tool as a metaphor, perhaps, but one with no less transformative intention, energy, or impact. The opening lines of the Finnish epic novel of the 20th century, *Here Under the Northern Star*, sound a parallel, culturally and geographically resonant ambition: "In the beginning, there was the swamp, Jussi (the diminutive of Juhani) and the hoe".[20] Bear in mind that in writing, Pallasmaa writes with the dictate of Milan Kundera in his mind – that a writer writes always to the ideal reader, but also always to himself – working therefore with both sincere optimism and honest directness.[21] This suggests that Pallasmaa works to clarify issues of architectural, philosophical and cultural importance for himself – to clear and cultivate the swamp, so to speak – with the extended hope that such work will be of further sustaining benefit to others.

This emphasis on the exploration and strengthening of self-identity through art and architecture is a resounding theme in Pallasmaa's essays, lecturing, teaching

7. Juhani Pallasmaa with Alberto Perez-Gomez and Steven Holl in the latter's office in New York in 1994, at the time of collaboration on Questions of Perception.

8. Library/Conference room of Juhani Pallasmaa Architects, Helsinki. The glass table was designed by Pallasmaa.
Photo Rauno Träskelin.

and design work. *The Eyes of the Skin* amplifies this theme through an insistence on a fully embodied and sensory architecture. The search for self-identity, however, is not a search for ego-centred self-expression – precisely the opposite. A more general imperative – the reconciliatory task of architecture – is also outlined as the ultimate poetic, personal and social, responsibility of the architect. It is an imperative Pallasmaa has sounded many times, many ways, but the call remains constant: 'Architecture's task is to articulate and express the essence of our lived world and to enable us to dwell in this world'.[22]

Apertures

Pallasmaa is now 87 years old, and announced his retirement from active design practice in 2020 to concentrate his energies on writing, lecturing and teaching. For many in the architectural communities of the Nordic countries, and for that number of European and North American sympathisers to the Finnish architectural cause, he is a representative figure – yet one whose work and voice even at this stage paradoxically has not been adequately exhibited and heard. The publication and reception since 1996 of *The Eyes of the Skin* clearly have provided increasing academic opportunities, and Pallasmaa has pursued a relentless lecturing and teaching schedule far outside Finland for almost three decades – at a pace equivalent perhaps only to the legendary touring of Muddy Waters, BB King and Chuck Berry (all musicians he admires, by the way, along with the jazz greats). But it is a little known, and little-discussed, fact that he sat on the Pritzker Prize Jury from 2008 to 2014, part of that time together with his good friend, the Australian architect Glenn Murcutt.

In his home country, however, while Pallasmaa is regarded as a 'phenomenon', the sheer amount of productivity and positions of responsibility in which he has succeeded in the Finnish architectural culture over the last

9. Chair, prototype, laminated plywood and carbon fibre and chromed spring steel, 1991. Source: From Rauno Träskelin.

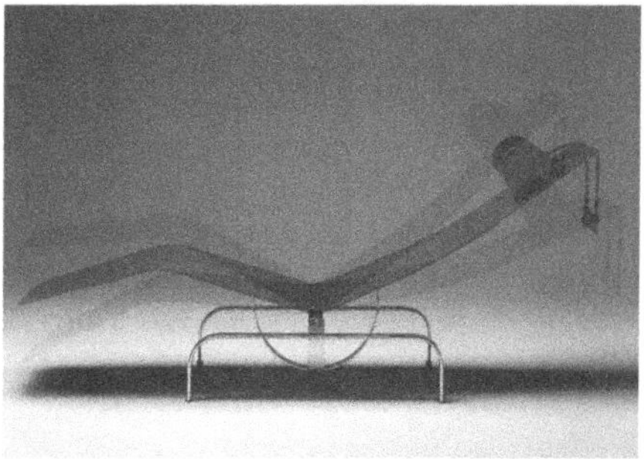

10. Adjustable reclining chair, prototype, 1994. Laminated plywood and carbon fibre, chromed spring steel base, leather head rest. Source: From Rauno Träskelin.

sixty years may not offer an adequate explanation. His has been an architectural life of fascinating versatility and surprisingly complementary roles, in which the strength of his protean intellect has paralleled an intense commitment to the making of an intimate architecture.

An existential geometry describing the substance of Pallasmaa's life might well be configured by a circle; a perimeter of circumstances, consistently expanding, but always with reference to the central point of his homeland, and to the central idea of *home*. 'In the visual arts in general and in architecture in particular the basic forms dominate: the circle, the square, the triangle, and the basic orientation and numbers. The circle, for instance, is a symbol of the self, expressing all the dimensions of the psyche, including the man–nature relationships'.[23] Home, the point of origin, that intimate inhabitation of house and landscape, functions as both psychological foundation and metaphorical description for Pallasmaa's work and thought. Simultaneously, the deep consciousness of his upbringing and culture has allowed the architect to move in widening arcs towards a deepening knowledge of the world beyond Finland, and towards a more profound understanding of art and architecture. An understanding of that circle of circumstances might best be framed by a series of apertures opening onto selected biographical moments.

Born in 1936 in pre-war Finland, as a young boy Pallasmaa was sent to his maternal grandfather's farm on the central Finnish plains to be out of harm's way during the long wartime years. Pallasmaa saw his soldiering father perhaps only every five or six months; the boy's grandfather and the vitality of the farm centred his life and he came thereby to know the value of simple things:

> 'I was the only boy in the entire dispersed village, and I spent my endlessly long days inventing pastime activities around the house and in the nearby forests, or observing the manifold chores of my aged but wise grand-dad. I admired his

diligence, and his multifarious skills and self-assurance; no work seemed insurmountable to him . . . I cannot recall anyone ever having been asked: can you do this? Mastering everything necessary was considered self-evident in farm life. The skills of the farmer were not theoretical knowledge learned through reading, but embodied and tacit wisdom, skills learned and remembered by muscles through observation and imitation . . . I can no longer conjure up a clear picture of the plank table in my grand-dad's kitchen (which served as the living room), but I can still imagine myself sitting beside it and reliving this focal point of a rural cottage, the binding force of our family circle and its occasional visitors'.[24]

The essential experience of this family circle, this home, remains in Pallasmaa's bones:

'Regardless of having in lived in eight houses, I have had only one experiential home in my childhood; my experiential home seems to have travelled with me and constantly transformed into new physical shapes as we moved . . . I recall vividly the sense of home, the feeling of returning home from a skiing trip in the darkness of a cold winter evening. The experience of home is never stronger than when seeing the windows of the house lit up in the dark winter landscape and sensing the invitation of warmth warming your frozen limbs'.[25]

11. Adjustable light fitting, 1986. Painted steel plate, steel base.
Source: From Rauno Träskelin.

12. Outdoor light fitting, 1998, for Kiasma Museum of Modern Art in Helsinki designed by Steven Holl.
Source: From Rauno Träskelin.

Following Finland's difficult conclusion to the Second World War, the family returned to southern Finland and eventually to Helsinki. As Pallasmaa recounts, his grandfather's influence continued in another, clearly artistic direction:

> 'At the age of fourteen, I inherited my paternal grandfather's oil painting equipment and quite a lot of oil paints. In the general poverty of the period after the war this felt luxurious and certainly strengthened my interest in painting and drawing; I had drawn obsessively already as a kid. If I had not known how difficult it was to make one's living as an artist, I could have become a painter . . .'[26]

As a 17-year-old American Field Service exchange student, Pallasmaa ambitiously travelled from Helsinki, first by boat across the Gulf of Finland to Stockholm – where he saw a television for the first time in a shop window – and then eventually across the Atlantic, to the United States, to the similarly flat and frigid landscapes of Minneapolis, to a year in an American high school, where he experienced not only the material and spiritual paradox that is America, but also won a state championship in cross-country skiing and a school prize for dancing the jitterbug. The initial American visit would be the first of many, in fact, and indeed, Pallasmaa estimates that he has spent more time in the United States than in any other country outside of Finland.

After finishing high school in 1957, Pallasmaa applied for entrance into the Faculty of Architecture at the then Helsinki Institute of Technology – still located then in a grand neo-classical structure on Hietalahdentori at the

13. Moduli 225 summer house system designed by Kristian Gullichsen and Juhani Pallasmaa, 1968-72. First prototype in Kinkamo. Photo Kaj Lindholm.

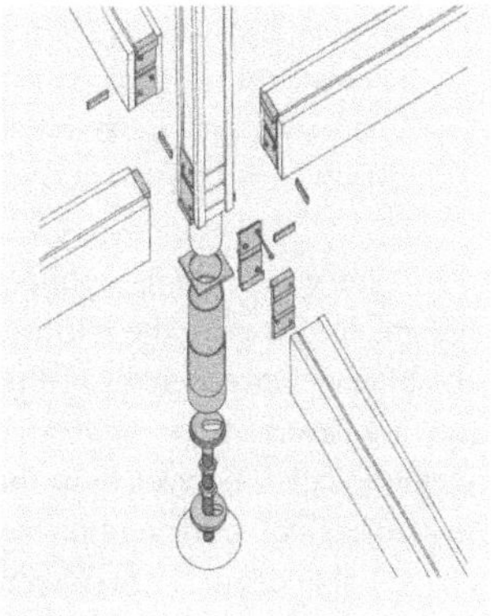

14. Moduli 225, standard joint details.

western end of Helsinki's Bulevardi (the Aalto-designed Otaniemi campus in Espoo of what would be the Helsinki University of Technology was under construction). In the post-war era, still characterised by economic austerity measures, he recalls being mesmerised by the original perspective drawings by Eliel Saarinen that adorned the corridor walls of the Faculty:

> 'As I was accepted into the Faculty of Architecture in Helsinki in 1957, I felt extremely privileged to be permitted entry to a new and different world, the world of artistic ideas and beauty. I did not think of my craft as a profession or a source of livelihood; I saw architecture as a mental position through which to experience the world meaningfully. Looking at Eliel Saarinen's original drawings along one of the corridors of the Faculty of Architecture set a fire in anybody's soul. Learning became a burning desire and in the post-war scarcity fed the imagination'.[27]

As a young graduated architect, fresh from an education gained under the tutelage of Finnish rationalists Aulis Blomstedt and Aarno Ruusuvuori in the late 1950s and early 1960s, Pallasmaa and his classmates attempted to understand their identity and professional role in an architectural culture dominated by the 'oak tree' figure of Alvar Aalto, and in a larger context, in the years surrounding the Paris Spring of 1968:

> 'There was a strong opposition between those of the "rationalist" school of thought and Aalto's 'Academy', but these tensions originated in the generation of Aalto. There was also a lot of ideological theater about Aalto's persona and genius which appeared unacceptable in the idealist democratic atmosphere of the 1960s . . . we not only had a strong social conscience, we believed in a universal, anonymous, international and democratic architecture for everybody. None of us were members of any political party, but we projected a politically oriented idealism. We believed that architecture held the answer to many social and political problems'.[28]

The vocal young architect upheld the primacy of rational thought in design, emphasising the importance of information and technology, opposing the bureaucratic excesses of the state. He would write at the time: 'Design is moving away from individual supervision and intuition to collective methodological control, from the design of separate sites to general systems and structures, and from immutable and ultimate design to disposable, changing and variable design'.[29] Architecture, in Pallasmaa's opinion at the time, was not 'a mystical attribute of space, but organization, the arrangement of facts. Actually, the word "beautiful" should be replaced by "right". For then art is the skill of doing right'. Such words would subsequently take on altogether different meanings. In 1968, at the age of 33, Pallasmaa was elected Rector of the Institute of Industrial Arts in Helsinki, elected by the 1300 students themselves after a succession of academic disturbances. His first action in this position of authority was to speak at a solidarity meeting of students in support of striking Finnish steel workers.

Yet in 1972, following his tenure as rector, Pallasmaa departed Finland entirely for Africa, in particular, for Ethiopia, where he assumed the responsibilities of an associate professor in architecture at the Haile Selassie I University in Addis Abeba for two and half years, under the auspices of the Finnish development aid program. The period was one of a self-imposed political exile and a transforming one for the maturing architect. His idealistic belief in the redemptive powers of rationalistic design, technology and building standardisation in his home country had already been disillusioned by the brutalising takeover of the building process by the Finnish construction companies. The control of pre-fabricated production, he observed, resulted in a tragic exclusion of quality, of human content, from the urgent needs for housing. In Africa, Pallasmaa rediscovered directly the meaning of the social content of architecture, as well as the advantage of small-scale modular systems in solving architectural commissions under drastically different conditions of culture and technology. Given the revolutionary moment in Ethiopia at time, the university was often closed; Pallasmaa readily accepted architectural commissions, among them an art museum for the university, housing, a multipurpose hall for the public health college in Gondar and a leprosy village for 150 families. Pallasmaa recalls that when the leprosy village was completed, the authorities determined that its quality was too high for the original inhabitants and re-purposed it for municipal workers.

The experience catalysed the architect's understanding of the cultural, environmental and psychological elements in his evolving architectural philosophy.

> 'My experiences in Ethiopia in the early 1970s disillusioned my confidence in rationality, in the unquestioned benefits of technology and ideas of universality. I became interested in anthropological, structuralist and eventually psychoanalytical writings. The writings of Erich Fromm and Herbert Marcuse were particularly important, and made me understand the essence of collective psychic phenomena. Anton Ehrenzweig's two books on the unconscious dimensions of artistic creativity and experience gave, perhaps, the most important single impulse to my way of thinking'.[30]

Combined with these readings, the African experience struck deep chords within Pallasmaa's consciousness and awakened an awareness of the possible role of archetypes, dreams and memories in art and architecture. The intellectual and emotional debt to the diverse cultural experiences of the African continent

15. Prototype house for the settlement of 150 leprosy families in Ambo, Ethiopia. The project was designed by Pallasmaa and his students at the Haile Sellassie I University in Addis Abeba in 1972–1974. The project was funded by the German Red Cross. Photo Juhani Pallasmaa.

16. Project for the Swedish School in Addis Abeba by Pallasmaa, 1973.

is undeniable in his subsequent writings and lectures. At the same time, the politicised dimensions of the commissions in Ethiopia were disillusioning for the young architect.

The interest in the psychological and the biological bases of spatial perception and the visual arts dominated Pallasmaa's thoughts upon his return to Finland in the mid-1970s. As Exhibition Director for the Museum of Finnish Architecture, he had ample opportunity to materially clarify the effects of his African experience through the design of numerous temporary exhibitions. Subsequently, during a five-year term as Director of the Museum, Pallasmaa internationalised the Museum's activities, with displays of work by Tadao Ando, Alvaro y Siza, Daniel Libeskind and American architectural drawings in an attempt to broaden the cultural outlook of the Museum. The Museum's yearbook, *Abacus*, became a forum for the examination of national and international architectural issues. His own contributions to the yearbook reflected his growing awareness of anthropological, linguistic and psychological issues, for example: 'The deep-structure meetings unconsciously aroused in the architectural experience are memories and associations connected with the synaesthetic mental images of early childhood, spatio-kinetic experience and collective archetypes'.[31]

Pallasmaa left the Museum in 1983, and put these ideas to the test with a growing number of independent design projects, beginning with his own apartment and continuing through thoroughly detailed designs for Marimekko and the Rovaniemi Art Museum. These projects of the 1980s were in many ways extensions of the principles worked out in exhibition design. The tactile was stressed over the sheerly visual, beginning with door handles, softened edges, consideration of materials, surfaces and light, and space was imbued with both proportional ordering and material sensibilities. By 1986, on the verge of

17. Three pieces of abstracted studies of staircases for an installation of 26 variations, cast in bronze and variously patinated, in an exhibition of three painters, a composer and an architect at the Helsinki City Art Hall, 1998.
Source: From Rauno Träskelin.

18. The grave marker of the atheist father of the architect. Cast and patinated bronze, 1968.
Source: From Rauno Träskelin.

an intense period of design commissions, Pallasmaa confirmed his shift in thinking in quoting Aalto's well-known statement concerning the depth of rationalisation in modern architecture and the new directions of the movement: '. . .the fault is that the rationalization has not gone deep enough. Instead of resisting the rationalist approach, the latest phase of modern architecture is trying to channel rational methods away from the technical sphere and into that of humanism and psychology'. His observation that 'it seems that Finnish architects in general are now engaged in materialising Aalto's programme of expanding a rational attitude to the psychological sphere of design' was both thinly veiled self-observation and a declaration of emergent intentions.[32]

Indeed, in 1985, Pallasmaa wrote an essay entitled "The Geometry of Feeling" for *Arkkitehti, the Finnish Architectural Review* (*The Architectural Review* would subsequently republish it in its full English-language version).[33] As he describes it, "only while writing this essay I became aware of phenomenology as a line of philosophical enquiry, and I added a short chapter on this philosophical approach in my essay".[34] But such a tentative initiative would soon expand and deepen.

In the early 1990s, with a growing number of larger-scale commissions and a growing office staff, Pallasmaa was appointed first professor (of the Basic Course in Architecture) and then Dean of the Faculty of Architecture at the Helsinki University of Technology. The academic appointments, while gratifying and resonant with the lineage of his mentors Blomstedt and Ruusuvuori, more importantly provided a platform from which to reinvigorate the theoretical dimension of the architecture curriculum, simultaneously attaching these poetic considerations to the material aspects of the building. Pallasmaa argued for a reworking of the idea of an architectural education, for a radical poetic of architecture, in which theory informs praxis, in which the satisfaction of function includes the awareness of the psychological dimensions of design, in which orders of material, structure, light and space accumulate towards a metaphysical experience. These ambitions for the curriculum and the Faculty also were aimed at overcoming the conventional perception of Finnish architecture as entirely pragmatic and resistant to theoretical statements or written speculations on the nature of architecture. And, too, well aware of the currents flowing through architectural education through his many visits to other schools, Pallasmaa sought to position the Faculty more prominently in the larger world of architectural education – but by deepening its Finnish identity.

Throughout these years, while elsewhere in the architectural world debates centred on a 'post-modern' architecture constituted by a superficial historicism or an equally superficial 'deconstructivism' in architecture, Pallasmaa consistently argued in his published writings and in public forums for an alternative reinvigoration of the philosophy and practice of the discipline. Such perspectives and essays found an initial international audience through the support of the British journal *The Architectural Review* and its long-time editor, Peter Davey, himself a great friend to Finnish architecture and a vigorous advocate for a more authentic contemporary architecture.

Pallasmaa's perspective was 'radical' in the sense that he called for a renewed understanding of architecture's ontology; the point of view being that architecture cannot disassociate itself from its metaphysical and existential basis:

> 'Our culture identifies the world of ideals and the everyday, and thus nullifies the function of art as mediator between the two . . . art must stir a consciousness of the metaphysical dimension superseding the everyday . . . The job of architecture is not to beautify or "humanise" the world of everyday fact, but to open a view into the second dimension of our consciousness, the reality of dreams, images and memories'.[35]

The architect was interpolating towards what might be called a metaphysical house, one of specific primary architectural images, elements and details:

> 'The house is composed by the architect as a system of spatial hierarchies and dynamics, structure, light, colour, etc., whereas home is structured around a few foci of behavior and symbolization: a front (front-yard, façade, the urban set-up), entry window, hearth, stove, table cupboard, bath, bookcase, furniture, family treasures, memorabilia. . .'[36]

It is against this backdrop of thinking, writing, teaching and practising that *The Eyes of the Skin* is first conceived, written and published in 1995–1996. Both Steven Holl, in his short preface to the book's second edition, and Pallasmaa in his own introduction included here, review the circumstances that brought the book into being. Holl's proposal to Pallasmaa and Pérez-Gómez that they join him in the 1993 A + U Special Edition entitled *Questions of Perception* obviously catalyses the perspectives and associations for all three.[37] For Pallasmaa, it is clear, however, that the ideas, research and concerns expressed so forcefully in *The Eyes of the Skin* had been fermenting for some time, and while the book can be read as an ambitious counterpoint to current events in architecture at the time, the book possesses a more important and lasting value when read as Pallasmaa's attempt to crystallise his attitudes, perceptions and insights for a longer duration.

Poetics

Pallasmaa's built work, produced over the last 50 years, threads throughout Helsinki, Finland, and into the world. Scattered among the Finnish archipelago in the Gulf of Finland are a series of small summer houses, including the architect's own hut, each site-specific experiments in material and detail. In Helsinki, his work registers in the city at a variety of scales, from a graceful set of bridges and pedestrian walks in the urban Ruoholahti neighbourhood to a subtle Market Hall restoration; from the understated, forest-green city telephone kiosks (now practically disappeared from the city streets!) and refuse containers to intimate, reinvigorated commercial courtyards; from restrained, elegant shop designs to finely detailed apartment interiors; from the street

19. Siida, The Sámi Lapp Museum and Northern Lapland Visitor Center, Inari, 1990–1998.
Photo Rauno Träskelin.

20. Korundi Cultural Center, Rovaniemi, Lapland, 1984–1986/2008–2011. The Concert Hall.
Source: From Rauno Träskelin.

lights and walkways surrounding Holl's Kiasma Museum of Contemporary Art to the 250-metre interior court of the Eastern Center shopping mall and Helsinki's Kamppi Center, a multi-storey complex of shops, housing, public transportation services and public squares.

In Kuopio, a regional capital in eastern Finland, an arc and chord courthouse addition; in Rovaniemi, on the Arctic Circle, a light-filled art museum shaped from the brick shell of a former bus depot, animated in its first phase by skilfully inserted and elegant details and in its second, most recent phase by an intimate chamber music hall, the colouration of which was designed in collaboration with the artist Jorma Hautala (the latter Pallasmaa's last publicly scaled work). In Inari, far above the Arctic Circle, an ethnographic museum for the Sami people of Lapland stands, aptly named SIIDA ('homestead' in the Sami language), a building design addressing complex issues of cultural representation, natural light, geography and climate.

Overseas, his Finnish Cultural Institute graces the Rue des Ėcoles, near the Sorbonne in Paris, a smoothly finished 'jewel-box' of interlocking volumes and spaces inside a former theatre. The Finnish Embassy in Beijing displays administrative quarters, a garden and a sauna, intertwining Finnish identity with deference to the host country's architectural traditions. And at the Cranbrook Schools in Michigan, long allied with Finnish architecture and design, an arrival area for the campus interweaves columns, paving stones, landscape, curving bronze panels, lighting and appeals to the cosmos into the Cranbrook fabric.

Throughout the work, a belief in the bodily experience of architecture upholds 'the tactile over the visual' and acknowledges as well a metaphysical

21. Finnish Institute, Rue des Écoles, Paris, 1986–1991. In collaboration with Roland Schweitzer and Sami Tabet, Paris.

22. Arrival Plaza, Cranbrook Academy, Bloomfield Hills, Michigan, 1994. In collaboration with Dan Hoffman and the Cranbrook Architecture Studio. Photo Balthazar Korab.

dimension to the task of building. The emphasis on the totality of design at all scales – through a graceful, sophisticated combination of geometry, materials, craftsmanship and detail – resonates throughout both his thought and work. Architecture is subsumed by a more complete process of design, one in which the tactile experience of space, light and material is balanced against the intellectual ordering of form through geometry and structure. Space and structure are rendered minimally, leaving a field for the elaboration of material. A certain palpable quality, a subtle eroticism, hovers over many elements. Inhabitants and visitors are seduced into such experience by the gift of the designed objects themselves – sensually curved door handles and drawer pulls are offered to the hand and fingers, for example. There is evident pleasure in the crafting of materials, both luxurious and simple, such as a coil of stainless steel, carved blocks of rusted steel, brass handles and layered plywood.

As with his ambitions for our experience of reading *The Eyes of the Skin*, Pallasmaa's intent in his designs is to slow down our experience of the designed space; it is an effect achieved by the thoughtful placement of architectural elements, by the careful use of coloured surfaces, by the introduction of shafts and washes of natural light from subtly placed roof lights, clerestories and framed wall openings, by the considered juxtaposition of materials, by the subtle imposition in ordering geometries in both plan and section and by the intense concentration on the precise crafting of each specific component and detail. The result is a 'collage', but one in which what is left to chance is the individual sensory experience alone, the subjective relationships and linkages created by the participation of those entering into the space, and their tactile memories. It

23. Summer studio of Tor Arne, painter, Vänö Islands, South Western Archipelago of the Gulf of Finland. Built of stones collected from the site. Source: Juhani Pallasmaa.

24. Two-family house Enarvi, Helsinki, 1972. The facade elements are made of plastics. Source: From Kari Hakli.

is the slowed passage of time that allows the tactile experience to resonate within one's consciousness long after departing from the design: the memory of granite disc or colonnade, a sweeping curve of tile and wall, a stair of an attenuated steel structure, a continuous succession of perforated door, wall and ceiling panels. A simple quietude, a calm reflection born of one's intimate discovery of an underlying spatial order, is animated by the appeal of the sensual use of materials and the comprehension of the craftsmanship of each element.

As his design career was succeeded by a dedication to writing and teaching, Pallasmaa travelled and lectured more and more often, usually to a full auditorium of entranced architecture students, professors, and professionals. In those, too, as with his buildings and writings, time slowed and acquired a palpable density. Throughout presentations often of several hundred stunning images – which usually form a second narrative to the spoken text – he dwelled on the essential tasks of art, architecture and education in our culture. In a darkened hall, his lecture would rise in tone and slow in pace to close with a central emphasis, quite often similar to this:

> The duty of education is to cultivate and support the human abilities of imagination and empathy, but the prevailing values of culture tend to discourage fantasy, suppress the senses, and petrify the boundary between the world and the self. Education in creativity today has to begin with a questioning of the absoluteness of the world, and the expansion of the boundaries of the self. The main object of artistic education is not in the principles of artistic making, but in the personality of the student and his or her image of themselves and the world. The idea of sensory training is nowadays connected solely with artistic education proper, but the refinement of sensory sensitivity and sensory thinking has an irreplaceable value in many other areas of human activity. I want to say more: the education of the senses and the imagination is necessary for a full and dignified life.[38]

Witnessing these lectures over many years, Pallasmaa's words always deeply resonated with audiences – whether of architecture students or professionals in other disciplines – and often led first to an appreciative, meditative silence and then an animated set of questions.

Since at least 1985 – the publication of "The Geometry of Feeling" – and certainly since the first 1996 publication of *The Eyes of the Skin*, Pallasmaa's work and thought has often been cited as an example of architectural phenomenology in anthologies of architectural theory, of philosophy applied into architectural thinking. The classifications are easy to understand, but simplistic – as simplistic as the labels of "Finnish minimalist" or "Nordic regionalist". The origins of Pallasmaa's work are layered, diverse and emerge from a more general humanistic tradition, as this introduction proposes, and Pallasmaa himself avoids any claim of being either a philosopher or a phenomenologist, due to his lack of formal education in the discipline and the philosophical method. "I am an amateur in this field", he declares, "(but) have read countless books by philosophers out of my personal interest in the enigma of human existence and the essence of knowledge".[39] He insists on his position as an architect working from an empirical, humanist stance: "I would rather say that my current view of architecture and art is parallel with what I understand the phenomenological stance to be. My "phenomenology" arises from my experiences as an architect, teacher, writer and collaborator with numerous fine artists, as well as my experiences of life in general".[40]

Pallasmaa is fond of quoting Bachelard's reference to the Dutch phenomenologist J H van den Berg's argument, "Painters and poets are born phenomenologists", as well as Merleau-Ponty's similar question, "How could a painter or a poet express anything other than his encounter with the world?" In response, and on the basis of his experiences, Pallasmaa asserts that as an architect, he too is a "born phenomenologist" – and encourages this belief among all architects: ". . . in my view, an architect is bound to explore and express this very same encounter (with the world). I believe that I am an architect primarily for the reason that this craft offers particularly essential and meaningful possibilities of touching the boundaries of one's self and the world, and experiencing how they mingle and fuse into each other".[41]

The Eyes of the Skin can perhaps be read, then, as another "gentle manifesto" in architectural thinking – but with far less emphasis on "complexity" or "contradiction" in architectural form. Pallasmaa does not aim for, or believe in, a prescriptive architectural theory; his approach, he says, is "in accordance with Edmund Husserl's notion of phenomenology as "pure looking", an innocent and unbiased encounter with phenomena, in the same manner that a painter looks at a landscape, a poet seeks a poetic image for a particular human experience – an architect imagines an existentially meaningful space".[42] Such existential concentration is the focus of Pallasmaa's insights: "Architecture is fundamentally existential in its very essence, and it arises from existential experience and wisdom rather than intellectualised and formalized theories. We can only prepare ourselves for our work in architecture by developing a distinct sensitivity and awareness for architectural phenomena".[43]

The Eyes of the Skin embodies this existential task, and encourages the development of such sensitivities. But although without prescription, the book proposes more than just diagnosis. Pallasmaa's approach is open-handed and open-ended, an authentically "open-source" for the consideration, conception and construction of a meaningful, sustaining architecture. *The Eyes of the Skin* proposes a renewed and invigorated education of the architect, perhaps as familiar to Vitruvius as it might have been to Semper, a reassertion of the

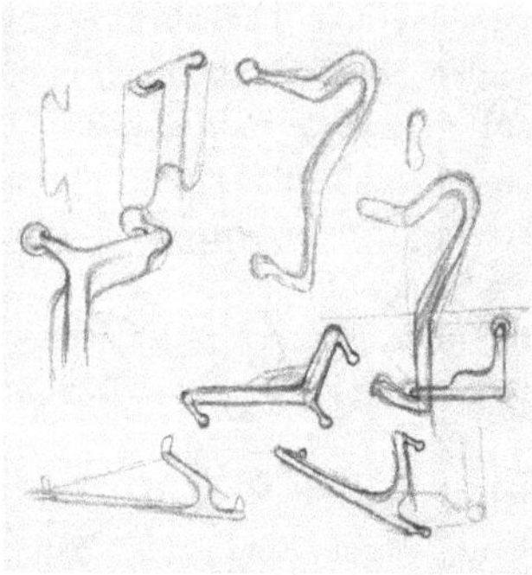

25. Sketches for door pulls, late 1980s.

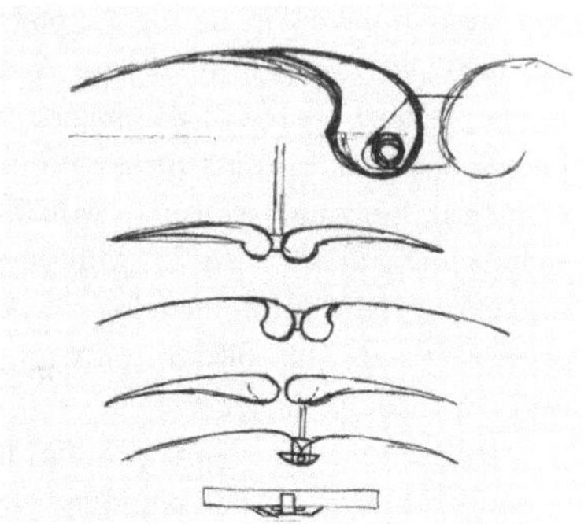

26. Sketches for light fixtures, early 1990s.

"poetics" inherent in the very meaning of the original words *education* and *architect*. Pallasmaa is emphatic on this poetic and ultimately optimistic mission:

> As educators we often use the notion "poetics" when speaking of the finest architectural qualities. At the face of the common utility and vulgarity of construction today this may sound pretentious, but I see as the fundamental task of architecture the mediation between the world and ourselves, history, present and future, human institutions and individuals, and between the material and the spiritual. This is nothing short of a poetic calling. As the settings of our lives are losing their human meaning, it is the task of art and architecture to re-mythicize, re-sensualize and re-eroticize our relationship with the world. Again, the question is about the poetic dimension of life. I do not consider the search for the poetic essence of architecture as a romantic or unrealistic endeavour, but as an absolute necessity. Simply, humanity is lost when life loses its echo in the deep historicity and spirituality of existence. Architecture can strengthen and maintain our grasp of the world and ourselves, and support humility and pride, curiosity and optimism.[44]

A door handle, a handshake, a conversation, an encounter: such is this small book.

NOTES

FOREWORD

1 Steven Holl, Juhani Pallasmaa and Alberto Pérez-Gómez, *Questions of Perception: Phenomenology of Architecture*, Special Edition, A+U Publishing (Tokyo), July 1994.

2 Steen Eiler Rasmussen, *Experiencing Architecture*, MIT Press (Cambridge, MA), 1959.

3 Maurice Merleau-Ponty, *The Visible and the Invisible*, Northwestern University Press (Evanston, IL), 1968, pp 148–9.

INTRODUCTION: TOUCHING THE WORLD

1 James Turrell, 'Plato's Cave and Light Within', in Mikko Heikkinen (ed), *Elephant and Butterfly: Permanence and Change in Architecture*, 9th Alvar Aalto Symposium (Jyväskylä), 2003, p 144.

2 Ashley Montagu, *Touching: The Human Significance of the Skin*, Harper & Row (New York, NY), 1986, p 3.

3 A notion of Johann Wolfgang von Goethe, as referred to in ibid, p 30.

4 Ludwig Wittgenstein, 'MS 112 46: 14.10.1931,' in GH von Wright (ed), *Ludwig Wittgenstein – Culture and Value*, Blackwell (Oxford), 2002, p 24e.

5 See, for example, Arnold H Modell, *Imagination and the Meaningful Brain*, MIT Press (Cambridge, MA; London), 2003, and Mark Johnson, *The Meaning of the Body: Aesthetics of Human Understanding*, University of Chicago Press (Chicago, IL; London), 2007.

6 See Anton Ehrenzweig, *The Psychoanalysis of Artistic Vision and Hearing: An Introduction to a Theory of Unconscious Perception*, Sheldon Press (London), 1975.

THE EYES OF THE SKIN, PARTS 1 AND 2

1 As quoted in Brooke Hodge (ed), *Not Architecture But Evidence That It Exists: Lauretta Vinciarelli – Watercolors*, Harvard University Graduate School of Design (Harvard), 1998, p 130.

2 Friedrich Nietzsche, *Thus Spake Zarathustra*, Viking Press (New York), 1956, p 224.

3 Richard Rorty, *Philosophy and the Mirror of Nature*, Princeton University Press (Prinecton, NJ), 1979, p 239.

4 Jorge Luis Borges, *Selected Poems 1923–1967*, Penguin (London), 1985, as quoted in Sören Thurell, *The Shadow of A Thought: The Janus Concept in Architecture*, School of Architecture, The Royal Institute of Technology (Stockholm), 1989, p 2.

5 As quoted in Richard Kearney, 'Maurice Merleau-Ponty', in Richard Kearney (ed), *Modern Movements in European Philosophy*, Manchester University Press (Manchester; New York, NY), 1994, p 82.

6 Heraclitus, Fragment 101a, as quoted in David Michael Levin (ed), *Modernity and the Hegemony of Vision*, University of California Press (Berkeley and Los Angeles, CA), 1993, p 1.

7 Plato, *Timaeus*, 47b, as quoted in Martin Jay, *Downcast Eyes: The Denigration of Vision in Twentieth-Century French Thought*, University of California Press (Berkeley and Los Angeles, CA), 1994, p 27.

8 Georgia Warnke, 'Ocularcentrism and Social Criticism', in Levin (1993), *op cit*, p 287.

9 Thomas R Flynn, 'Foucault and the Eclipse of Vision', in Levin (1993), *op cit*, p 274.

10 Peter Sloterdijk, *Critique of Cynical Reason*, trans Michael Eldred, as quoted in Jay (1994), *op cit*, p 21.

11 As referred to in Steven Pack, 'Discovering (Through) the Dark Interstice of Touch', *History and Theory Graduate Studio 1992–1994*, McGill School of Architecture (Montreal), 1994.

12 Levin (1993), *op cit*, p 2.

13 *Ibid*, p 3.

14 David Harvey, *The Condition of Postmodernity*, Blackwell (Cambridge), 1992, p 327.

15 David Michael Levin, 'Decline and Fall – Ocularcentrism in Heidegger's Reading of the History of Metaphysics', in Levin (1993), *op cit*, p 205.

16 David Michael Levin, *Ibid*, p 212.

17 Dalia Judovitz, 'Vision, Representation, and Technology in Descartes', in Levin (1993), *op cit*, p 71.

18 Levin (1993), *op cit*, p 4.

19 Friedrich Nietzsche, *The Will to Power*, Book II, trans Walter Kaufmann, Random House (New York, NY), 1968, note 461, p 253.

20 Max Scheler, *Vom Umsturz der Werte: Abhandlungen und Aufsätze*, as quoted in David Michael Levin, *The Body's Recollection of Being*, Routledge & Kegan Paul (London; Boston, MA; Melbourne; Henley), 1985, p 57.

21 Jay (1994), *op cit*.

22 Martin Jay, 'Sartre, Merleau-Ponty, and the Search for A New Ontology of Sight', in Levin (1993), *op cit*, p 149.

23 As referenced in Richard Kearney, 'Jean-Paul Sartre', in Kearney, *Modern Movements in European Philosophy*, *op cit*, p 63.

24 Jay (1994), *op cit*, p 149.

25 Sigfried Giedion, *Space, Time and Architecture: The Growth of a New Tradition*, 5th revised and enlarged edition, Harvard University Press (Cambridge, MA), 1997.

26 *Op cit.*, p. 376.

27 Martin Jay, 'Scopic Regimes of Modernity', in Hal Foster (ed), *Vision and Visuality*, Bay Press (Seattle, WA), 1988, p 10.

28 Merleau-Ponty describes the notion of the flesh in his essay 'The Intertwining – The Chiasm', in Claude Lefort (ed), *The Visible and the Invisible*, Northwestern University Press (Evanston, IL), 4th printing, 1992: 'My body is made of the same flesh as the world [. . .] this flesh of my body is shared by the world' (p 248); and, 'The flesh (of the world or my own) is [. . .] a texture that returns to itself and conforms to itself' (p 146). The notion derives from Merleau-Ponty's dialectical principle of the intertwining of the world and the self. He also speaks of the 'ontology of the flesh' as the ultimate conclusion of his initial phenomenology of perception. This ontology implies that meaning is both within and without, subjective and objective, spiritual and material. See Richard Kearney, 'Maurice Merleau-Ponty', in Kearney, *Modern Movements in European Philosophy*, *op cit*, pp 73–90.

29 As quoted in Hubert L Dreyfus and Patricia Allen Dreyfus, 'Translators' Introduction', in Maurice Merleau-Ponty (ed), *Sense and Non-Sense*, Northwestern University Press (Evanston, IL), 1964, p XII.

30 Maurice Merleau-Ponty, 'The Film and the New Psychology', in *ibid*, p 48.

31 Italo Calvino, *Six Memos for the Next Millennium*, Vintage Books (New York, NY), 1988, p 57.

32 Martin Heidegger, 'The Age of the World Picture', in Martin Heidegger (ed), *The Question Concerning Technology and Other Essays*, Harper & Row (New York, NY), 1977, p 134.

33 Harvey, *op cit*, pp 261–307.

34 *Ibid*, p 293.

35 As quoted in *ibid*, p 293.

36 Edward T Hall, *The Hidden Dimension*, Doubleday (New York, NY), 1969.

37 Walter J Ong, *Orality and Literacy: The Technologizing of the World*, Routledge (London and New York, NY), 1991.

38 *Ibid*. p 117.

39 *Ibid*. p 121.

40 *Ibid*, p 122.

41 *Ibid*. p 12.

42 As quoted in Jay (1994), *op cit*, p 34.

43 As quoted in *ibid*, pp 34–5.

44 Gaston Bachelard, *The Poetics of Space*, Beacon Press (Boston, MA), 1969, p XII.

45 Leon Battista Alberti, as quoted in Levin (1993), *op cit*, p 64.

46 As quoted in Jay (1994), *op cit*, p 5.

47 Le Corbusier, *Precisions*, MIT Press (Cambridge, MA), 1991, p 7.

48 Pierre-Alain Crosset, 'Eyes Which See', *Casabella*, 531–532 (1987), p 115.

49 Le Corbusier (1991), *op cit*, p 231.

50 *Ibid*, p 227.

51 Le Corbusier, *Towards a New Architecture*, Architectural Press (London) and Frederick A Praeger (New York, NY), 1959, p 164.

52 *Ibid*, p 191.

53 Walter Gropius, *Architektur*, Fischer (Frankfurt; Hamburg), 1956, pp 15–25.

54 As quoted in Susan Sontag, *On Photography*, Penguin (New York, NY), 1986, p 96.

55 Le Corbusier (1959), *op cit*, p 31.

56 Alvar Aalto, 'Taide ja tekniikka' [Art and Technology] (1955), in Alvar Aalto and Göran Schildt (eds), *Alvar Aalto: Luonnoksia [Sketches]*, Otava (Helsinki), 1972, p 87 (trans Juhani Pallasmaa).

57 As quoted in Jay (1994), *op cit*, p 19.

58 Harvey, *op cit*, p 58.

59 Fredric Jameson, as quoted in *ibid*, p 58.

60 Maurice Merleau-Ponty, *The Phenomenology of Perception*, as quoted in Iain McGilchrist (ed), *The Master and His Emissary: The Divided Brain and the Making of the Western World*, Yale University Press (New Haven, CT), 2009, p 184.

61 Levin (1993), *op cit*, p 203.

62 Sontag, *op cit*, p 7.

63 *Ibid*, p 16.

64 *Ibid*, p 24.

65 From a conversation with Professor Keijo Petäjä in the early 1980s; the source is unidentified.

66 Hans Sedlmayr, *Art in Crisis: The Lost Centre*, Hollis & Carter (London), 1957.

67 Maurice Merleau-Ponty, 'Cézanne's Doubt', in Merleau-Ponty (1964), *op cit*, p 19.

68 Martin Jay, 'Scopic Regimes of Modernity', in Hal Foster (ed), *Vision and Visuality*, Bay Press (Seattle, WA), 1988, p 18.

69 *Ibid*, p 16.

70 *Ibid*, p 17.

71 David Michael Levin, *The Opening of Vision: Nihilism and the Postmodern Situation*, Routledge (New York, NY; London), 1988, p 440.

72 *Ibid*.

73 Ong, *op cit*, p 136.

74 Montagu, *op cit*, p XIII.

75 With its 800,000 fibres and 18 times more nerve endings than in the cochlear nerve of the ear, the optic nerve is able to transmit an incredible amount of information to the brain, at a rate which far exceeds that of all the other sense organs. Each eye contains 120 million rods which take in information on roughly five hundred levels of lightness and darkness, while more than seven million cones make it possible for us to distinguish among more than one million combinations of colour. Jay (1994), *op cit*, p 6

76 Edward Relph, *Place and Placelessness*.

77 Kearney, *Modern Movements in European Philosophy*, *op cit*, p 74.

78 Maurice Merleau-Ponty, *Phenomenology of Perception*, Routledge (London), 1992. p 203.

79 *Ibid*, p 225.

80 Kent C Bloomer and Charles W Moore, *Body, Memory, and Architecture*, Yale University Press (New Haven, CT; London), 1977, p 44.

81 *Ibid*, p 105.

82 *1Ibid*, p 107.

83 Gaston Bachelard, *The Poetics of Reverie*, Beacon Press (Boston, MA), 1971, p 6.

84 On the basis of experiments with animals, scientists have identified 17 different ways in which living organisms can respond to the environment.
Jay (1994), *op cit*, p 6.

85 Bloomer and Moore, *op cit*, p 33.

86 The anthropology and spiritual psychology based on Rudolf Steiner's studies of the senses distinguishes 12 senses: touch; life sense; self-movement sense; balance; smell; taste; vision; temperature sense; hearing; language sense; conceptual sense; and ego sense. Albert Soesman, *Our Twelve Senses: Wellsprings of the Soul*, Hawthorn Press (Stroud, Glos), 1998.

87 Quoted in Victor Burgin, 'Perverse Space', as quoted in Beatriz Colomina (ed), *Sexuality and Space*, Princeton Architectural Press (Princeton, NJ), 1992, p 233

88 Jay, as quoted in Levin (1993), *op cit*.

89 Stephen Houlgate, 'Vision, Reflection, and Openness: The "Hegemony of Vision" from a Hegelian Point of View', in Levin (1993), *op cit*, p 100.

90 As quoted in Houlgate, *ibid*, p 100.

91 As quoted in Houlgate, *ibid*, p 108.

92 Merleau-Ponty (1964), *op cit*, p 15.

93 As quoted in Montagu, *op cit*, p 308.

94 As referenced by Montagu, *ibid*.

95 Le Corbusier (1959), *op cit*, p 11.

96 Bachelard (1971), *op cit*, p 6.

97 Kakuzo Okakura, *The Book of Tea*, Kodansha International (Tokyo; New York, NY), 1989, p 83.

98 Edward S Casey, *Remembering: A Phenomenological Study*, Indiana University Press (Bloomington and Indianapolis, IN), 2000, p 172.

99 As quoted in Judovitz, in Levin (1993), *op cit*, p 80.

100 Maurice Merleau-Ponty, *The Primacy of Perception*, James M Edie (ed), Northwestern University Press (Evanston, IL), 2000, p 162.

101 Le Corbusier (1959), *op cit*, p 7.

102 Merleau-Ponty (1964), *op cit*, p 19.

103 Jun'ichirō Tanizaki, *In Praise of Shadows*, Leete's Island Books (New Haven, CT), 1977, p 16.

104 Alejandro Ramírez Ugarte, 'Interview with Luis Barragán' (1962), in Enrique X de Anda Alanis, *Luis Barragán: Clásico del Silencio*, Collección Somosur (Bogota), 1989, p 242.

105 Ong, *op cit*, p 73.

106 Adrian Stokes, 'Smooth and Rough', in *The Critical Writings of Adrian Stokes*, Volume II, Thames & Hudson (London), 1978, p 245.

107 Steen Eiler Rasmussen, *Experiencing Architecture*, MIT Press (Cambridge, MA), 1993.

108 *Ibid*, p 225.

109 Karsten Harries, 'Building and the Terror of Time', *Perspecta: The Yale Architectural Journal* (New Haven, CT), 19 (1982), pp 59–69.

110 Cyril Connolly, *The Unquiet Grave: A Word Cycle by Palinurus*, Curwen Press for Horizon (London), 1944.

111 Quoted in Emilio Ambasz, *The Architecture of Luis Barragán*, The Museum of Modern Art (New York, NY), 1976, p 108.

112 Bachelard (1969), *op cit*, p 13.

113 Diane Ackerman, *A Natural History of the Senses*, Vintage Books (New York, NY), 1991, p 45.

114 Rainer Maria Rilke, *The Notebooks of Malte Laurids Brigge*, trans MD Herter Norton, W.W. Norton & Company (New York, NY; London), 1992, pp 47–8.

115 Rainer Maria Rilke, *Auguste Rodin*, trans Daniel Slager, Archipelago Books (New York, NY), 2004, p 45.

116 Martin Heidegger, 'What Calls for Thinking', in *Martin Heidegger, Basic Writings*, Harper & Row (New York, NY), 1977, p 357.

117 Bachelard (1971), *op cit*, p XXXIV.

118 *Ibid*, p 7.

119 Marcel Proust, *Kadonnutta aikaa etsimässä, Combray* [Remembrance of Things Past, Combray], Otava (Helsinki), 1968, p 10.

120 Gaston Bachelard, *The Poetics of Space*, Beacon Press (Boston, MA), 1968, p 34.

121 Stokes, *op cit*, p 243.

122 Source unidentified.

123 Stokes, *op cit*, p 316.

124 Tanizaki, *op cit*, p 15.

125 Bachelard (1971), *op cit*, p 91.

126 *Ibid*, p 15.

127 'From Eclecticism to Doubt', dialogue between Eileen Gray and Jean Badovici, *L'Architecture Vivante, 1923–33*, Autumn-Winter 1929, as quoted in Colin St John Wilson, *The Other Tradition of Modern Architecture*, Academy Editions (London), 1995, p 112.

128 Tadao Ando, 'The Emotionally Made Architectural Spaces of Tadao Ando', as quoted in Kenneth Frampton, 'The Work of Tadao Ando', in Yukio Futagawa (ed), *Tadao Ando*, ADA Edita (Tokyo), 1987, p 11.

129 In the mid-19th century, the American sculptor Horatio Greenough gave with

this notion the first formulation on the interdependence of form and function, which later became the ideological cornerstone of Functionalism. Horatio Greenough, *Form and Function: Remarks on Art, Design, and Architecture*, Harold A Small (ed), University of California Press (Berkeley and Los Angeles, CA), 1966.

130 Henri Bergson, *Matter and Memory*, Zone Books (New York, NY), 1991, p 21.

131 Casey, *op cit*, p 149.

132 Alvar Aalto, 'From the Doorstep to the Common Room' (1926), in Göran Schildt, *Alvar Aalto: The Early Years*, Rizzoli International Publications (New York, NY), 1984, p 214–18.

133 Fred and Barbro Thompson, 'Unity of Time and Space', *Arkkitehti, The Finnish Architectural Review*, 1981, issue 2, pp 68–70.

134 As quoted in 'Translators' Introduction' by Hubert L Dreyfus and Patricia Allen Dreyfus in Merleau-Ponty (1964), *op cit*, p XII.

135 As quoted in Bachelard (1969), *op cit*, p 137.

136 Henry Moore, 'The Sculptor Speaks', in Philip James (ed), *Henry Moore on Sculpture*, MacDonald (London), 1966, p 62.

137 *Ibid*, p 79.

138 Merleau-Ponty (1964), *op cit*, p 17.

139 See, for instance, Hanna Segal, *Melanie Klein*, The Viking Press (New York, NY), 1979.

140 Richard Lang, 'The Dwelling Door: Towards a Phenomenology of Transition', in David Seamon and Robert Mugerauer, *Dwelling, Place and Environment*, Columbia University Press (New York, NY), 1982, p 202.

141 Louis I Kahn, 'I Love Beginnings', in Alessandra Latour (ed), *Louis I Kahn: Writings, Lectures, Interviews*, Rizzoli International Publications (New York, NY), 1991, p 288.

142 Jeff Malpas in his lecture at the Understanding and Designing Place Symposium at the Tampere University on 3 April, 2017.

143 Jean-Paul Sartre, *What Is Literature?*, Peter Smith (Gloucester), 1978, p 3.

144 *Ibid*, p 4.

145 Alvar Aalto, 'Rationalism and Man' (1935), in Alvar Aalto and Göran Schildt (eds), *Alvar Aalto: Sketches*, trans Stuart Wrede, MIT Press (Cambridge, MA; London), 1978, p 48.

146 Frank Lloyd Wright, 'Integrity', in *The Natural House*, 1954. Published in *Frank Lloyd Wright: Writings and Buildings*, selected by Edgar Kaufmann and Ben Raeburn, Horizon Press (New York, NY), 1960, pp 292–3.

A DOOR HANDLE, A HANDSHAKE: AN INTRODUCTION TO JUHANI PALLASMAA AND HIS WORK

Portions of the text are excerpted from: Peter MacKeith, 'A Full and Dignified

Life', *Archipelago: Essays on Architecture*, Rakennustieto (Helsinki), 2006, pp 214–34.

1 Juhani Pallasmaa, as quoted in 'An Architectural Confession' (2010 unpublished manuscript provided to the author).

2 *Ibid.*

3 *Ibid.*

4 Alvar Aalto, 'The Humanizing of Architecture' (1940), in Alvar Aalto and Göran Schildt (eds), *Alvar Aalto: Sketches*, trans Stuart Wrede, MIT Press (Cambridge, MA), 1985, p 77.

5 Steen Eiler Rasmussen, *Experiencing Architecture*, MIT Press (Cambridge, MA), 1959.

6 Useful references to Sigurd Lewerentz are: Janne Ahlin, *Sigurd Lewerentz, Architect*, MIT Press (Cambridge, MA), 1989; Adam Ed Caruso, *Sigurd Lewerentz: Two Churches*, Gingko Press (Hamburg), 1999; Nicola Flora, Paolo Giardiello and Gennaro Postiglione (eds), *Sigurd Lewerentz*, Phaidon (London), 2006.

7 Key publications by Christian Norberg-Schulz, include: *Intentions in Architecture*, MIT Press (Cambridge, MA), 1968; *Existence, Space and Architecture*, Praeger Publishers (New York, NY), 1974; *Genius Loci: Towards a Phenomenology of Architecture*, Rizzoli (New York, NY), 1984.

8 Useful references to Sverre Fehn are: Per Olaf Fjeld, *Sverre Fehn: The Thought of Construction*, Rizzoli (New York, NY), 1983; Per Olaf Fjeld, *Sverre Fehn: The Pattern of Thoughts*, Monacelli (New York, NY), 2009.

9 Useful references for Colin St John Wilson are: Colin St John Wilson, *Architectural Reflections: Studies in the Philosophy and Practice of Architecture*, Butterworth-Heinemann (London), 1992; Colin St John Wilson, *The Other Tradition of Modern Architecture: The Uncompleted Project*, Academy Editions (London), 1995; Roger Stonehouse and Eric Parry, *Colin St John Wilson: Buildings and Projects*, Black Dog Publishing (London), 2007.

10 Key publications by Adrian Stokes, include: *The Quattro Cento: and, Stones of Rimini*, Pennsylvania State University Press (University Park, PA), 2002 (originally published 1932 and 1934 respectively); *Smooth and Rough*, Faber & Faber (London), 1951; *The Image in Form*, Penguin (London), 1972.

11 Key writings by Kenneth Frampton, include: 'Towards a Critical Regionalism: Six Points for an Architecture of Resistance', in Hal Foster (ed), *The Anti-Aesthetic: Essays on Postmodern Culture*, Bay Press (Port Townsend, WA), 1983, pp 16–30; *Studies in Tectonic Culture: The Poetics of Construction in Nineteenth and Twentieth Century Architecture*, MIT Press (Cambridge, MA), 2001; *Labour, Work and Architecture*, Phaidon Press (London), 2002; *Modern Architecture: A Critical History (World of Art)*, Thames & Hudson (London), 4th edition, 2007.

12 Gaston Bachelard, *The Poetics of Space*, Beacon Press (Boston, MA), 1969.

13 Useful references to Steven Holl and the design of Kiasma, the Museum of

Contemporary Art, Helsinki are: *KIASMA, Museum of Contemporary Art, Helsinki*, Gingko Press (Berkeley, CA), 1999; Annette LeCuyer, 'Iconic Kiasma', *The Architectural Review*, August 1998, pp 46–53; Peter MacKeith, 'The Helsinki Museum Competition', *Competitions* 4, issue 2 (Summer 1994), pp 44–51.

14 Alberto Pérez-Gómez, *Architecture and the Crisis of Modern Science*, MIT Press (Cambridge, MA), 1983.

15 Key writings by Gaston Bachelard, include: *Earth and Reveries of Will: An Essay on the Imagination of Matter*, trans Kenneth Haltman, Dallas Institute of Humanities and Culture (Dallas, TX), 3rd edition, 2002; *Air and Dreams: An Essay on the Imagination of Movement*, trans Edith R Farrell and C Frederick Farrell, Dallas Institute of Humanities and Culture (Dallas, TX), 3rd edition, 1988; *Water and Dreams: An Essay on the Imagination of Matter*, trans Edith R Farrell, Dallas Institute of Humanities & Culture (Dallas, TX), 3rd edition, 1999; *The Psychoanalysis of Fire*, trans Alan CM Ross, Beacon Press (New York, NY), 1987; *The Poetics of Reverie: Childhood, Language, and the Cosmos*, trans Daniel Russell, Beacon Press (New York, NY), 1971. Key writings by Maurice Merleau-Ponty, include: *The Structure of Behavior*, trans Alden Fisher, Beacon Press (Boston, MA), 1963; *Phenomenology of Perception*, trans Colin Smith, Humanities Press (New York, NY), 1962; *Sense and Non-Sense*, trans Hubert Dreyfus and Patricia Allen Dreyfus, Northwestern University Press (Evanston, IL), 1964; *The Visible and the Invisible, Followed by Working Notes*, trans Alphonso Lingis, Northwestern University Press (Evanston, IL), 1968; *The Prose of the World*, trans John O'Neill, Northwestern University Press (Evanston, IL), 1973.

16 Juhani Pallasmaa, *The Thinking Hand: Existential and Embodied Wisdom in Architecture*, AD Primer, John Wiley & Sons (Chichester), 2009; Juhani Pallasmaa, *The Embodied Image: Imagination and Imagery in Architecture*, AD Primer (ed), John Wiley & Sons (Chichester), 2011.

17 Pallasmaa, 'An Architectural Confession' (2010), *op cit*.

18 *Ibid*.

19 Franz Kafka, letter to Oskar Pollak, 27 January 1904; cited from Max Brod (ed), *Briefe, 1902–1924*, Schocken (New York, NY), 1958.

20 Väinö Linna, *Under the North Star* (Finnish: *Täällä Pohjantähden alla*, original publication 1959), trans Richard Impola, Aspasia Books (Beaverton, OR, Canada), 2001.

21 Milan Kundera, *Romaanin taide (The Art of the Novel)*, WSOY (Helsinki), 1986, p 165.

22 Pallasmaa, 'An Architectural Confession' (2010), *op cit*.

23 Marja-Riitta Norri, 'The World of Juhani Pallasmaa', in Juhani Pallasmaa and Marja-Riitta Norri, *Architecture in Miniature: Juhani Pallasmaa, Finland*, The Museum of Finnish Architecture (Helsinki), 1991, p 3. Published in conjunction with the Alvar Aalto Pavilion exhibition of Pallasmaa's work at the 5th International Exhibition of Architecture of the Venice Biennale, 8 September to 6 October 1991.

24 Juhani Pallasmaa, in conversation with Peter MacKeith, 2005. See 'Landscapes: Juhani Pallasmaa in Conversation with Peter MacKeith', *Encounters: Architectural Essays*, Rakennustieto (Helsinki), 2005, pp 6–22.

25 Juhani Pallasmaa and Marja-Riitta Norri, *Architecture in Miniature: Juhani Pallasmaa, Finland, op. cit.*

26 Pallasmaa, 'An Architectural Confession' (2010), *op cit.*

27 Juhani Pallasmaa, in conversation with Peter MacKeith, 2011.

28 Juhani Pallasmaa, in conversation with Peter MacKeith, 2005. See 'Landscapes: Juhani Pallasmaa, in conversation with Peter MacKeith' (2005), *op cit.*

29 Norri, 'The World of Juhani Pallasmaa', *op cit.*

30 Juhani Pallasmaa, in conversation with Peter MacKeith, 2005. See 'Landscapes: Juhani Pallasmaa, in Conversation with Peter MacKeith' (2005), *op cit.*

31 Juhani Pallasmaa, 'The Two Languages of Architecture: Elements of a Bio-Cultural Approach to Architecture', *Abacus 2, The Yearbook of the Museum of Finnish Architecture*, The Museum of Finnish Architecture (Helsinki), 1980, pp 57–90.

32 Alvar Aalto, 'The Humanizing of Architecture', *op cit.*

33 Juhani Pallasmaa, 'The Geometry of Feeling: A Look at the Phenomenology of Architecture', *Arkkitehti, The Finnish Architectural Review*, 1985, issue 3, pp 44–9.

34 Pallasmaa, 'An Architectural Confession' (2010), *op cit.*

35 Norri, 'The World of Juhani Pallasmaa', *op cit.*

36 Juhani Pallasmaa, 'Identity, Intimacy and Domicile: Notes on the Phenomenology of Home', *Arkkitehti, The Finnish Architectural Review*, 1994, issue 1, pp 14–25.

37 Steven Holl, Juhani Pallasmaa and Alberto Pérez-Gómez, *Questions of Perception: Phenomenology of Architecture,* Special Edition, A+U Publishing (Tokyo), July 1994.

38 Juhani Pallasmaa, lecture at Washington University in St Louis School of Architecture, 2005.

39 Pallasmaa, 'An Architectural Confession' (2010), *op cit.*

40 *Ibid.*

41 Pallasmaa, 'An Architectural Confession' (2010), *op cit.*

42 *Ibid.*

43 *Ibid.*

44 Juhani Pallasmaa, in conversation with Peter MacKeith, 2011.

INDEX

5th Alvar Aalto Symposium (Jyväskylä, Finland, 1991) ix, 69

A+U ix, 3, 81
Aalto, Alvar 22, 28, 40, 44, 55, 61, 65, 67, 68, 76, 79
Acoustic intimacy 42–43
Action images 54–55
Alberti, Leon Battista 20, 28–30
Althusser, Louis 14
Ambo, Ethiopia: prototype house *78*
Ando, Tadao 54, 78
Angelico, Fra: *Annunciation* 55
Apertures 72–81
Aquinas, St Thomas 10
Architectural Review, The 79, 80
Aristotle 10
Arkkitehti, the Finnish Architectural Review 79
Arnaud, Noël 55
Asplund, Erik Gunnar 65, 67, 68

Bachelard, Gaston 20, 34, 38, 46, 50–52, 69, 85
  The Poetics of Space 69
Baroque 28, 30, 43
Barragán, Luis 46, 51
Barthes, Roland 14
Bataille, Georges 14
Benjamin, Walter 25
Berenson, Bernard 36
Bergson, Henri 14, 54
Berkeley, George 35
Berry, Chuck 72
Björkhagen church, Stockholm, Sweden 68
Blomstedt, Aulis 68, 76, 80
Bloomer, Kent C 34
Bodily identification 55–56
Bonnard, Pierre 36
Booth, Gotthard 25
Borges, Jorge Luis 9, 69
Bosch, Hieronymus 28
Brodsky, Joseph 69
Bruegel, Pieter, the Elder 28
Brunelleschi, Filippo 67

Calvino, Italo 16, 60
Caravaggio 39
Carleton University, Canada 69
Casa Batlló, Barcelona 50
Casey, Edward S 38, 54
Certeau, Michel de 17
Cézanne, Paul 30, 39, 56
Connolly, Cyril: *The Unquiet Grave* 46
Contemporary architecture 26–28
Cooper Union School of Architecture, New York 69
Cranbrook Academy, Bloomfield Hills
  Architecture Studio 69
  Michigan 82, *82*
Cubists 30

Davey, Peter 80
Debord, Guy 14
Deconstructivism 80
Derrida, Jacques 14, 15
Desargues of Lyon, Gérard 19
Descartes, René 14
Dewey, John 33
DL James House, Carmel, California 51
Dostoevsky, Fyodor 60
Dutch paintings (17th-century) 28

Eastern Centre shopping mall, Helsinki 82
Egyptian architecture 43
Ehrenzweig, Anton 77
Expressionism 61

Fallingwater, Pennsylvania 36
Febvre, Lucien 19

The Eyes of the Skin: Architecture and the Senses, Fourth Edition. Juhani Pallasmaa.

Fehn, Sverre 68, 69
Finnish Cultural Institute, Paris 82
Finnish Embassy, Beijing 82
Finnish Institute, Paris *82*
Fjeld, Per Olaf: *The Thought of Construction* (1984) 68
Foucault, Michel 15
Frampton, Kenneth 68
Frankfurt School 68
Fromm, Erich 77
Functionalism 23

Gaudi, Antonio 50
Gestalt 6, 7, 23, 54, 61
Gibson, James J 35
Giedion, Sigfried; *Space, Time and Architecture* 15
Giotto 67
Goethe, Johann Wolfgang von 9, 36
Gothic architecture 43
Grave marker *79*
Gray, Eileen 52, 68
Great Peristyle, Karnak, Egypt 44
Greek architecture 20, 24
Greeks, ancient 11
Greek thought 10, 24
Greene, Charles and Henry 51
Gropius, Walter 21
Gullichsen, Kristian *75*

Haile Selassie I University, Addis Abeba, Ethiopia 77, *78*
Hall, Edward T 17
Harvey, David 11, 16, 24
Hautala, Jorma 82
Hegel, Georg Wilhelm Friedrich 35
Heidegger, Martin 15, 68
Hejduk, John 69
Helsinki
  Market Hall 81
  Ruoholahti 81
Helsinki Institute of Technology: Faculty of Architecture 75
Helsinki Museum of Contemporary Art ix, 69
Helsinki University of Technology
  Faculty of Architecture 75, 79
  Otaniemi campus, Espoo 76

Heraclitus 10
Hitchcock, Alfred 60
Holl, Steven 3, 61, 69, *72*, *74*, 81, 82
Holl, Steven, Pallasmaa, Juhani and Pérez-Gómez, Alberto: *Questions of Perception: Phenomenology of Architecture* ix, 3, *72*, 80–81
Husserl, Edmund 85

Impressionists 30
Institute of Industrial Arts, Helsinki 77
Irigaray, Luce 14

Jacobsen, Arne 65
Jameson, Fredric 24
Japanese thinking 55
Jay, Martin 30
  Downcast Eyes: The Denigration of Vision in Twentieth-Century French Thought 14
Jefferson, Thomas 70
Juhani Pallasmaa Architects, Helsinki: Library/conference room 70, 72

Kafka, Franz 71
Kahn, Louis 30, 50, 58
Kamppi Centre, Helsinki 82
Kearney, Richard 33
Keller, Helen 47
King, BB 72
Kinkamo, Finland *75*
Klein, Melanie 56
Knowledge 10–14
Korundi Cultural Center, Rovaniemi, Lapland *81*
Kundera, Milan 71
Kuopio, Finland 82

Lacan, Jacques 14
Land artists 30
Lang, Richard 56
Le Corbusier 21, 38, 39, 44, 47, 61
Levinas, Emmanuel 14
Levin, David Michael 11, 13, 24
  The Opening of Vision: Nihilism and the Postmodern Situation 30
Lewerentz, Sigurd 68

Lewin, David Michael: *Modernity and the Hegemony of Vision* 11
Libeskind, Daniel 69, 78
'Life-enhancing' architecture 4
Loss of plasticity 20–23
Lyotard, Jean-François 14

Mandrou, Robert 19
Marcel, Gabriel 55
Marcuse, Herbert 77
Marimekko 78
Marimekko Shop in Helsinki *70*
Materiality/time 25–28
Matisse, Henri 36
McGill University, Montreal 69
Meier, Richard 61
Melnikov House, Moscow 44, 47
Melnikov, Konstantin 44
Memory and imagination, spaces of 60–61
Mendelsohn, Erich 61
Merleau-Ponty, Maurice ix, x, 6, 9, 14, 15, 24, 33, 35, 36, 38, 39, 56, 69, 85
Michelangelo 60
Mies van der Rohe, Ludwig 23
Mimesis, of body 56–60
Modernism 14, 21
Modernity and the Hegemony of Vision (Lewin) 11
Moduli 225
  industrially produced summerhouse system ix, *75*
  standard joint details *75*
Moholy-Nagy, László 21
Montagu, Ashley 4, 31
Moore, Charles W 34
Moore, Henry 55
Multi-sensory experience 34–39
Murcutt, Glenn 31, 72
Muscle and bone images 51–54
Museum of Finnish Architecture, Helsinki 78
  Abacus (yearbook) 78

Nakamura, Toshio ix
Narcissistic eye 16–17
Natural materials 25
Nietzsche, Friedrich 9, 14
Nihilistic eye 16–17
Norberg-Schulz, Christian 68

Ocularcentrism, critics of 14–16
Okakura, Kakuzo: *The Book of Tea* 38
Ong, Walter J 17 31, 42
Oral *vs.* visual space 17–20

Paimio Sanatorium, Finland 44
Pallasmaa, Juhani *72, 75*
  adjustable light fitting *74*
  adjustable reclining chair *73*
  age of four *66*
  age of seventy five *66*
  'An Architecture of the Seven Senses' 3
  carbon fibre and chromed spring steel *73*
  chair, prototype, laminated plywood *73*
  The Embodied Image: Imagination and Imagery in Architecture 7, 70
  exhibition, in Finland Pavilion *67*
  The Eyes of the Skin ix, 3, 4, 7, 10–62, 65–72, 81, 83–85
  Marimekko Shop in Helsinki *70*
  outdoor light fitting *74*
  prototypes for door handles *67*
  prototypes for drawer and door pulls *70*
  Rootedness: reflections for young architects 7
  sketches for door pulls *67, 86*
  sketches for light fixtures *86*
  staircases for installation *79*
  'The Geometry of Feeling' 79, 84
  The Thinking Hand: Existential and Embodied Wisdom in Architecture 7, 70
Pantheon, Rome 43
Pérez-Gómez, Alberto ix, 3, 69, *72,* 81
Piero della Francesca 67
Plato 10, 23
Poetics 81–86
'Polemics' series, Academy Editions 3
Post-Modernism 80
Pritzker Prize Committee 72
Proust, Marcel 50

Rasmussen, Steen Eiler ix, 42, 68
  Experiencing Architecture 42, 68
Relph, Edward: *Place and Placelessness* 33

Rembrandt van Rijn 39
Renaissance 10, 23, 28 30, 43
Retinal architecture 20–22
Rilke, Rainer Maria 46, 47, 69
The Notebooks of Malte Laurids Brigge 47
Rodin, Auguste 48
Rorty, Richard 9
Rovaniemi Art Museum and Concert Hall, Korundi, Rovaniemi ix, 81
Royal Danish Academy of Fine Arts, Copenhagen 3
Ruskin, John 50
Ruusuvuori, Aarno 68, 76, 80
Ryoan-ji Zen Garden, Kyoto, Japan 39

Saarinen, Eliel 65, 76
Salk Institute, La Jolla, California 50
San Francisco 60
Sartre, Jean-Paul 14, 60
Säynätsalo Town Hall, Finland 40
Scarpa, Carlo 51
Scent, spaces of 46–47
Scharoun, Hans 61, 68
Scheler, Max 14
Sedlmayr, Hans 26
Semper, Gottfried 85
Sense, architecture of 61–62
Serra, Richard 30
Shadows, significance of 39–40
SIIDA Sámi Lapp Museum, Inari, Northern Lapland *81,* 82
Silence, time and solitude 43–44
Siza, Alvaro y 78
Sloterdijk, Peter 10
Sontag, Susan 24
Spitz, René 35
Starobinski, Jean 23
Steiner, Rudolph 35
Stokes, Adrian 42, 50, 68
Stone surface 51
St Peter and St Mark church, Klippan, Sweden 68
St Petersburg, Russia 60
Summer studio, of Tor Arne, painter, Vänö Islands *83*
Sutherland, Graham 56

'Tactile values' 36
Tanizaki, Jun'ichirō 51
In Praise of Shadows 39
Third Man, The (film) 43
Thompson, Professor Fred 55
Timeless task, of architecture 62
Tintoretto 60
Touch, shape of 48
Turner, Joseph Mallord William 30, 36
Two-family house Enarvi, Helsinki *83*

Utzon, Jorn 68

Valéry, Paul 38
van den Berg, JH 85
van Eyck, Aldo 67
Vertigo (film) 60
Villa Savoye, Poissy, Paris, France 44
Villa Stein-de Monzie, Garches, France 47
Vision 10–13
Visual images, architecture of 24–25
Visual space, oral *vs.* 17–18
Vitruvius 85

Wartofsky, Marx W 21
Waters, Muddy 72
Welles, Orson 43
Western architectural theory 20
Wilson, Colin St John 68
Wittgenstein, Ludwig 5
Wright, Frank Lloyd 30, 36, 61, 62

Zumthor, Peter 61

PICTURE *CREDITS*

PART *ONE*

1 Out of copyright.

2 Luis Buñuel Estate © LBFI 2012; © Salvador Dali, Fundació Gala-Salvador Dalí, DACS, 2012.

3 Dziga Vertov/The Museum of Modern Art, New York/ Scala, Florence.

4 © Stiftung Preussische Schlösser und Gärten, Berlin-Brandenburg.

5 Magritte © ADAGP, Paris and DACS, London 2011.

6 Bayer © DACS 2011.

7 Corbusier © FLC/ADAGP, Paris and DACS, London 2011.

8 Photo: Juhani Pallasmaa.

9 © Ocean/Corbis.

10 © The Aulis Blomstedt Estate/ Severi Blomstedt.

PART *TWO*

11 © Kunsthistorisches Museum with MVK and ÖTM, Vienna.

12 Photo: Juhani Pallasmaa.

13 Photo: David Heald.

14 Photo: Juhani Pallasmaa.

15 © 2011 White Images/Scala, Florence.

16 © Jose Fuste Raga/Corbis.

17 © 2011 Photo Scala, Florence.

18 Museum of Finnish Architecture (Photo: István Rácz).

19 State Public Library, Ulan Bator, Mongolia.

20 Museum of Finnish Architecture (Photo: Heikki Havas).

21 Mairea Foundation (Photo: Rauno Träskelin).

The Eyes of the Skin: Architecture and the Senses, Fourth Edition. Juhani Pallasmaa.

22 The Museum of Modern Art, New York/Scala, Florence.

23 © Hélène Binet.

24 Mairea Foundation (Photo: Rauno Träskelin).

A DOOR HANDLE, A HANDSHAKE: AN INTRODUCTION TO JUHANI PALLASMAA AND HIS WORK

1 Photographer unknown.

2 Courtesy of Juhani Pallasmaa, private archive. Photo: Knut Thyberg.

3 Sketch: Courtesy of Juhani Pallasmaa, private archive.

4 Photo: Rauno Träskelin.

5 Photo: Rauno Träskelin.

6 Photo: Rauno Träskelin.

7 Courtesy of Juhani Pallasmaa, private archive.

8 Courtesy of Juhani Pallasmaa, private archive. Photo: Rauno Träskelin.

9 Photo: Rauno Träskelin.

10 Photo: Rauno Träskelin.

11 Photo: Rauno Träskelin.

12 Photo: Rauno Träskelin.

13 Photo: Kaj Lindholm.

14 Courtesy of Juhani Pallasmaa, private archive.

15 Courtesy of Juhani Pallasmaa, private archive.

16 Sketch: Courtesy of Juhani Pallasmaa, private archive.

17 Photo: Rauno Träskelin.

18 Photo: Rauno Träskelin.

19 Courtesy Juhani Pallasmaa Architects, Helsinki. Photo: Rauno Träskelin.

20 Photo: Rauno Träskelin.

21 Courtesy Juhani Pallasmaa Architects, Helsinki. Photo: Gérard Dufresne.

22 Courtesy Juhani Pallasmaa Architects, Helsinki. Photo: Balthazar Korab.

23 Photo: Juhani Pallasmaa.

24 Photo: Kari Hakli.

25 Sketch: Courtesy of Juhani Pallasmaa, private archive.

26 Sketch: Courtesy of Juhani Pallasmaa, private archive.